"A work that teaches us about love for other species, shows us that our lives are very similar to those of parrots, and that by learning from them, these birds can change us, and we can change the world."

- **Diana Pésole,** founder of the Association for the Conservation of Psittacines in Paraguay

"LoraKim Joyner is undoubtedly one of the most remarkable people I ever met. Her experiences in witnessing the deaths of parrots and humans in war-torn Central America left her suffering from post-traumatic stress when she returned to the USA. Yet, she was inspired to initiate, almost single handedly, truly remarkable parrot conservation projects in countries so violent or lawless that she risked her life daily to conserve the parrots she loved. Their populations were being plundered, bringing some species close to extinction. Amid so much tragedy, she discovered how connecting with birds could heal, bring joy, and grow resilience. Her strength and courage, then and now, are awe-inspiring. In this book, she describes her unique journey of recovery and discovery, based on her respect and passion for the natural world - and for human beings. Perhaps it could be described as a self-help book rather than one on birdwatching. However we name it, it is unique."

- **Rosemary Low,** author of avian books

"LoraKim Joyner's insights in *Birding for Life* are an insightful and valuable resource to anyone who shares this big, beautiful planet of ours. Birds may seem a small and insignificant piece of nature in the view of many, often taken for granted, but they are vital to biodiversity and, as Joyner's personal story reveals, to our own wellbeing and self-understanding as human beings and as a society in crisis. This book gives the reader a chance to connect deeply to Earth through the lens of birding and with practical exercises one can put to use in their own lives to offer moments of reflection and connection in our increasingly changing climate."

- Sarah D. Norton, PhD, author, and Convener for Education at the Foundation for Family and Community Healing

Praise for *Birding for Life*

"Packed full of practical wisdom and deep compassion, Dr. LoraKim Joyner's book is a timely, empathic guide. She identifies the ways our five forms of intelligence allow us to appreciate the interconnected beauty and wonder of the earth that we, birds, and other animals call home. *Birding for Life* is both guide and clarion call for urgent caring action to save ourselves and life on the planet."

- **Lori Gruen**, American philosopher, ethicist, author, and the William Griffin Professor of Philosophy at Wesleyan University

"In this extraordinary book, LoraKim Joyner brings us on a journey of inner and outer reflection, demonstrating that birds and all the beauty, tragedy, resilience, pain, freedom and loss of freedom represented in the culture of birds are reflected in our own human culture and in our hearts. Knowing, understanding, and valuing who birds are inspires us to explore our own place and purpose in the world we share, and to grow because of that experience. In this way, birding becomes a spiritual anchor and a practice in mindfulness, enabling us to embrace our own grace, depth, and worth as we do theirs."

- **Karen Windsor**, Executive Director, Foster Parrots, Ltd

"When LoraKim asked me to give a quick read to an early draft of her newest book, I had no idea it would change my listening skills and awareness of the birds I could hear and when I could hear none. My world took wings, and I finished the last page wishing for more as a converted birder."

- **Jane Arrowsmith Edwards**, editor, playwright, novelist, and novice birder

"It was a great joy to read my dear friend, colleague, and mentor's book *Birding for Life*. "For" as in perpetuating your life and "For" as in forever. This is a fun and emotional read, on a very personal level. LoraKim has an honest and wise voice and the experiences across joy and horror that legitimize and demystify our connections with nature no namby-pamby mumbo-jumbo but real, heartfelt human experience. Thank you, LoraKim, for giving us this gift."

- **Pat Latas**, artist, veterinarian for wildlife and avians, Co-chair IUCN SSC Wild Parrot Specialist Group

"If you are bird-curious, or early in your bird journey this book is the perfect guidepost to lead you deeper in. It highlights everything the bird-curious need to know about how birds can act as guides through a tumultuous world - internal or external- and how they bring us together in our grief, joy, and shared humanity as beings that inhabit Earth. I am grateful for the opportunity to share yet another reflection of her time across the Americas (and beyond) and appreciate how birds can help us take the punches and fully bear witness to the beauty that's always around us and within us."

- **Nicole Becich**, DVM, Association of Avian Veterinarians Conservation Committee Chair

"LoraKim Joyner reminds us that nature and the planet are at a precipice - and we need to change the way we're doing things. By saving the birds we save such a large and integral piece of our planet. This book inspires us to see avian life differently, pathing a road to hope."

- **Colet Abedi**, bestselling author

Praise and Explanation for the Cover of *Birding for Life*

"I would like to praise the lovely cover image. For those of you who are not familiar with the species depicted, they are the black vulture and the crested caracara. Both are fascinating, highly social and intelligent species in their own right. Both are considered to be sacred birds in many indigenous cultures. I personally have known and worked with members of both species and they are incredible, on a one-to-one basis.

The cover image is deeply meaningful in depicting interspecies affection. Love and care that is given freely between two very different species. They often meet at a carcass, as both enjoy carrion snacks; but there is no competition or aggression. Sometimes vultures feed baby caracaras. Vultures often have particular friends in the caracara families and sometimes choose to roost with them. There are numerous photos of these sweet interactions from across the vast area where these species overlap, including Florida, Texas and the desert southwest of the USA; Mexico; Central and South America.

We have a lot to learn from these amazing birds, and we should study and absorb those lessons seriously. I applaud the cover image and the message it shares. As an artist, I can testify how hard it is to tell a story and share concepts in a simple and beautiful image. This one does all that and more."

-**Pat Latas**, artist, veterinarian for wildlife and avians, Co-chair IUCN SSC Wild Parrot Specialist Group

Birding for Life

Birding for Life
How to Save Ourselves, Birds, and the Planet

LoraKim Joyner

 2025 © by LoraKim Joyner

One Earth Conservation, 2025
Birding for Life: How to Save Ourselves, Birds, and the Planet is made available under a Creative Commons Attribution - Non-Commercial - No Derivatives 4.0 License. For more information, please visit https://creativecommons.org/licenses/.

Published by One Earth Conservation
Edition 1.1 May 2025
ISBN: 979-8-9859414-1-8
Library of Congress Control Number: 2025939754
First Edition First Printing
www.oneearthconservation.org
info@oneearthconservation.org
+1 (718) 776-7284

Cover Design Copyright 2025 © by Rebecca Guenther at Near Bird Studios

Cover depicts a black vulture and a crested caracara, perched on a leafless branch, overlooking a mountain range whose colors are brightening in the sunrise. The black vulture is preening the crested caracara whose wings are up. These two birds show the wonder of multispecies relationships. Flying away from these birds are a flock of critically endangered yellow-naped parrots flying towards the sunrise.

All proceeds from sales directly support parrot conservation

To all the birds I have known

Contents

Preface – Guide to Birding for Life
1

Introduction – Birding Is for Life
7

Nesting Intelligence - Introduction to Five Natural Intelligences
21

Emotional Intelligence - Love Your Inner Bird
27

Social Intelligence - Don't Flip Them the Bird
65

Multispecies Intelligence – Be the Bird
89

Ecological Intelligence – Holy Bird Shit!
149

Spiritual Intelligence – Birds Beyond Words
177

Flying Free – Flying Lessons for Giving a Flock
193

In Conclusion – With Liberating Wings
227

Appendix – Feelings and Needs List
231

Acknowledgements
233

About One Earth Conservation
234

About the Cover – A Birding for Life Practice
235

About the Author
239

Preface
Guide to Birding for Life

*I pray to the birds.
I pray to the birds because they remind me of what I
love rather than what I fear.
And at the end of my prayers, they teach me how to listen.*
- Terry Tempest Williams[1]

As a child I thought God had it wrong. Raised a country Methodist in Tennessee, I had a moderate fear of hell and my father. When my parents prompted me to perform routine nightly prayers, I complied. I asked God to keep us all safe and let us be good. When my parents left the room, I looked out the window at the hickory tree spread against the night sky. Wonder, immensity, and humility filled the space of what I did not know how to say. God, according to my parents and Sunday school, presided over a human heaven, the reward for good behavior. This emphasis seemed oblivious to other species. With head bowed to the hickory and imaginary angel birds soaring over me, I whispered to God that if birds couldn't go to heaven, then I didn't want to go either.

As if in response, nightmares plagued my sleep from early childhood until age fifteen. Birds screamed at me, died, and dissolved into ashes. Violent monsters stalked me. The causes of my nightmares might have been anxious and controlling parents that believed in corporal punishment, my sense of unfairness of our family's patriarchal power structure, and the disappearing forests around our suburban home, combined with my particular sensitivities.

Before I was school age, I sought ease in the woods where I sang to the birds and trees. They were the friends I could count on, and they sang back. Years later, Madonna's song "Like a Prayer" expressed my childhood experiences.

> *Life is a mystery, everyone must stand alone*
> *I hear you call my name*
> *And it feels like home*
> *, I hear your voice*
> *Feels like flying*

When the nightmares finally stopped, my dreams sometimes brought joy. In one, I was in the woods looking for birds when an ivory-billed woodpecker flew into the tree above me. My heart sang. They're not extinct! They are with us! I awoke ecstatic and felt euphoric for days. Indeed, some of that euphoria took up permanent residence in me and informed me that my purpose in this world was to be witness to and help birds as much as I can.

I attended the University of California at Davis and received a Bachelor of Science in Avian Science and a Doctor of Veterinary Medicine. As a veterinarian I have worked only with birds — first with captive birds, mostly parrots in large collections. Their songs did not seem so bright, nor was mine at the sight of them in cages stacked high on shelves. Those cages sent me to Central America to help protect free-flying parrots from the twin threats of poaching and habitat loss.

Shortly after my first arrival in Guatemala, I contracted amoebic dysentery. Nauseous and dizzy, I stepped out for cooler air on a wooded path; that's when, for the first time, I saw free-flying parrots. Even with dysentery, the sight of them made me dance.

BIRDING FOR LIFE

I spent most of 1990-1995 in Guatemala. Civil war, strife, and violence tore through the region. My joy at working with parrots was mixed with sorrow at the rampant human need surrounding me. Birds and humans were both wracked by a culture of death and greed. I witnessed trauma upon trauma as if cages trapped not only the birds of the world, but also the oppressed, as well as conservationists like me.

I returned to the United States and took a job as an avian veterinarian at North Carolina State University's School of Veterinary Medicine. There, an agonizing thought played in my head: I had abandoned the parrots and people of Central America. Birds were one of my strongest connections to life, beauty, and hope, yet being with them in the wild also brought me pain, guilt, and post-traumatic stress disorder.

My earlier book, *Conservation in Time of War*, describes my journey to find my place amid this tragedy and beauty. In the process, I discovered how connecting with birds could heal, bring joy, and grow resilience. I found the path to returning to the frontlines of conservation.

This path led to studying at Vanderbilt Divinity School (1997-2000), to being ordained as a Unitarian Universalist minister, and to serving congregations for a decade. In 2010, I returned to Latin America to continue my efforts in conservation. Within my first year back, my work directed me to an Indigenous Miskito village in Honduras. At the start of our conservation season, most of the villagers circled around under tall pine trees where once hundreds of parrots had flown and now only a few could be found. I asked each person to offer a blessing or prayer for the work before us. When it was my turn, I began to recite Mary Oliver's poem, "Wild Geese." The villagers had never heard of wild geese, so I substituted them for macaws and the original places for ones they would know. Please forgive me, Mary Oliver. The poem begins:

You do not have to be good.
You do not have to walk on your knees
for a hundred miles through the jungle, repenting.
Meanwhile the macaws, high in the clean blue air,
are heading home again.

During the recitation of the poem, we heard the calls of five macaws, a rare family at a time when most chicks were poached before they could fly free. The macaws soared directly overhead with their beautiful wings spread against the sky. As they sang their deep cries, I finished the poem.

Many of us, including me, wept. The birds had told us that we belong. In fact, they always tell us that, but in that moment we were able to hear them. In that knowing, we committed ourselves once again to the life around and inside us.

The power of our connection to other species is a form of love that allows humans to work under extraordinary conditions, with extraordinary results. Since I began working there, Honduras has suffered a coup, had the highest murder rate in the world, had the highest death rate of environmentalists, and witnessed a massive emigration of children escaping violence and despair. Sadly, in 2014, not one scarlet macaw chick escaped poaching to fly free in our Honduran conservation area. Yet we persisted, and in 2016 and 2017 not one chick was poached for the wildlife trade.

Such successes tend to be temporary. Poaching continues, although at a significantly reduced rate, as does loss of habitat. But those of us who do conservation work are sustained by our connection to all of life. That connection fans our hopes and softens days of struggle like feathers brushing against our cheeks.

That connection and belonging are available to you, too. This calls for faith in the fact that even if you don't see a particular species or the abundance you hoped for, the beauty around us never dies.

That is also true of tragedy. Our task is to attend to the intricate weaving of beauty and tragedy, so that we may live for the benefit of all species. May we, with Terry Tempest Williams, pray to the birds, believe in their invocations and benedictions, remember our love more than our fears, and allow the birds to teach us how to listen.

Welcome to the community of birds and birders!

Notes

1. Williams TT. *Refuge: An Unnatural History of Family and Place.* Vintage: New York, NY. 1992.

Introduction
Birding Is for Life

If you have bought this book, return it. If you are reading this, shut the cover and go out and be with birds. If yet you persist, I warned you. Great beauty is found in more than words. Find such beauty in birds.

"Put a Bird on It"

A sketch on the comedy show *Portlandia* featured Fred Armisen and Carrie Brownstein entering a small boutique and saying, "Put a bird on it," about each item they saw. I thought this was hilarious because a bird decoration certainly attracts my attention.

Part of my attraction to Sufism as well is their symbol of a winged heart. Sufis believe birds are born twice: when laid, and when hatched. The Sufis interpret this as a metaphor, or evidence, for the possibility of a second human birth. One of Sufism's sacred texts is the *Conference of the Birds*, which I have read many, many times. Slap the image of a bird on just about anything, and I'm a sucker for it.

Is this book you're currently holding what the comedy show *Portlandia* was spoofing? Is it some woo-woo spirituality to which a false bird association has been tacked on? I do not think so. Birds have moved human spirits since times out of mind. If bird images are effective marketing tools, it's because birds are meaningful to so many people. "Birding," or birdwatching, is popular around the globe. During the COVID-19 pandemic in 2020 the ranks of birders soared and still continues to do so.[1] Of course, if something else – newts, elk, or koi; sycamore trees or slime mold; cloud types or soil strata; poetry or music or art or science; or your faith tradition; or whatever – is your entry point for gaining the awareness and resilience we need to heal Earth and our societies, then I applaud you. This book invites you to develop your sense of connection to birds and explore the healing potential of that connection for yourself and for our planet.

Beware of Consumerist Mindfulness

Birds are big business, in that billions of dollars are spent by consumers on bird books, observation equipment, tours, décor, and clothes, as is the mindfulness industry. Marketers intimate that you can buy your way to enlightenment with little effort. Countless mindfulness seminars, books, and assorted paraphernalia compete for customers. My own house happens to be full of bird figurines, meditation supplies, spirituality books, several pairs of binoculars, spotting scopes, and field guides. Birding apps also fill my phone. Some items are helpful, but none are necessary for mindfulness. Nor, of course, are they individually or collectively sufficient.

This book describes the practice of being with birds — beyond the tools, beyond even words, thereby losing the false sense of separation and instead embracing the moment. For that, nothing need be bought, not even this book.

BIRDING FOR LIFE

Reality Is Humbling

Undertaking this practice does not require having the right equipment, or being a good birder, or traveling far. Birding can be done for a few minutes at a time in your own backyard. The idea is to just slow down and appreciate the birds you see or hear. Some birders are competitive, but I recommend setting aside any such impulse to compare your birding experience to anyone else's. If birding were a competition, I would not do very well myself. Yes, I have had an obsession with birds my entire life, but I followed the path of becoming an avian veterinarian and then a minister, both of which are different skill sets than those of the most avid birders.

When I was nineteen, I nearly dropped out of college because no courses excited me. When I learned that the University of California at Davis offered a degree in Avian Sciences, I transferred there from my community college. Arriving in Davis before classes had begun, I visited the wild bird professor who invited me to join his graduate students for early morning birding. I didn't own a pair of binoculars. The professor lent me a small pair, and as the students started calling out names of birds and where they were located, I pretended I knew all about the birds they named. The truth was that I wasn't even seeing any birds, and I told the professor his binoculars were broken. He looked at me and flipped the binoculars over, so I could look through the correct end.

I wanted to quit right then, and the embarrassment haunted me until I graduated. That was not the last time my birding skills proved lacking. Watching birds does build confidence — not so much in knowing about birds, but in connecting to reality and nature — and you do not even have to be good at it! Getting out and sharing wonder, awe, and beauty with others enriches our body and soul. But first, get out there.

Reality Is Humbling and Uncomfortable

I am still not that hot at birdwatching, even when I am looking through the correct end of the binoculars, even though I'm a wildlife avian veterinarian specializing in parrot conservation. I have spent thousands of hours observing and counting birds – parrots, usually – because monitoring populations and noting basic behaviors are foundational for conservation. Yet when I am in the field conducting a parrot survey, it has happened more than once that my cohorts have asked incredulously, "You don't see or hear those parrots?" I am the expert dedicated to saving parrots, yet I struggle to identify and count them. This is humbling. Even as a young veterinarian working in Guatemala, I would miss parrots coming and going from the nest cavity. I would be sure that the pair was still in the tree cavity, only to have them fly in from somewhere else.

Why haven't I gotten better? It is true that I was born with one eye partially paralyzed, and it's hard to track moving objects, which often appear doubled. I also have a bad leg that makes balancing and quickly turning a challenge, especially when tracking birds. A few years ago, I learned I have had a 50% hearing loss for an unknown amount of time. I had cataracts removed, and I wear hearing aids now, which have helped. My point is that you do not have to be good at birding or have the optimal equipment in order to engage in birding as a mindfulness practice. Just paying attention to birds brings me more awe and wonder every year.

Birding for Life is the practice of seeing yourself as part of the flock. The flock constantly moves around you. Think of the beauty of a starling murmuration: There is safety in numbers for the starlings, as the undulation of the murmuration helps them avoid predators. Yes, life is out to get us, but our evolutionary spirit manifests in the beauty that we become by decentering ourselves. The "center" of a murmuration is elusive, constantly shifting, and not especially important anyway. Starlings have no inclination to be at the center, and we needn't either.

You will begin to feel welcomed on this planet and welcoming to others by watching birds with intent. Growing your awareness of birds and deepening your relationship with them facilitates greater acceptance of reality, which can sometimes be uncomfortable. But it is also how we build our compassion and connection.

Birds Are Everywhere. Well, Not So Much as They Used to Be

The crisis is ultimately not precisely about biodiversity. It is about restructuring our relationship as human beings with the natural world, and birds are an excellent place to start.
– Boria Sax in Avian Illuminations

Birds are an excellent support for a mindfulness practice because in most environments they are easily observable. They can show up in the most populated or degraded environments. When they are present, they are often visible, audible, or both. They grab our attention, which is a step towards a focused or mindful practice.

We also focus on birds because they are in danger.[2-6] In North America, there were 3 billion fewer birds in 2020 than in 1970. One-quarter of all birds are gone. Nineteen bird species have declined by 50 million or more during that time period. One-eighth of all bird species are globally threatened with extinction.[3] Their main threats include habitat destruction, agricultural expansion and deforestation, invasive species, and human hunting and trapping. These threats also affect another million species, including mammals, reptiles, and amphibians, as well as our overall ecosystem health. A catastrophic decline in biodiversity endangers a broad swath of both individual species and communities of species.

Birds, people, and the planet are in trouble, as birdwatching reminds us. Moreover, birding cultivates mindfulness that helps develop our resilience so the destruction around us does not debilitate our effective caring response. As in birding, in mindfulness and resilience there is no "perfection" to achieve. We must be kind to ourselves on the days that our thoughts are scattered or despairing.

Dying Birds Are Perfect

In the 1998 film *Thin Red Line*, a fictionalized account of United States' soldiers in the World War II Guadalcanal campaign, Private Train (John Dee Smith) comes across an injured parrot chick that was blasted from its tree home and says:

> "One man looks at a dying bird and thinks there's nothing but unanswered pain, that death's got the final word, it's laughing at him. Another man sees that same bird, feels the glory, feels something smiling through it."

The disappearance of bird species and their individual suffering, especially that of parrots, has been a great sorrow and motivator in my life. As a wildlife veterinarian working on front-line parrot conservation in the Americas for nearly four decades, I know what it's like to hold dying birds in my hand and have their existence slip from human ken. Each loss is a kick in my gut. There may be some glory smiling through something tragic, but many people, perhaps not even consciously, experience the disappearance of bird abundance and diversity as a diminution of the human spirit.

Grief, regret, and shared mourning, though necessary, are not enough. We must also be strong, joyful, and resilient. We must know the bird's unanswered pain, as we also "feel the glory, feel something smiling through it." This is not easy. I struggle to accept a bird's death as part of the beautiful whole. Yet I know more deeply by being with birds that all that has been and is before me in my days of parrot conservation, including the suffering and the loss, is a perfection. This perfection does not mean that I or any of us may retreat from striving to end suffering.

Solutions to suffering are varied and often complex. Strategies include reduced consumption, more sustainable production, less pollution and climate change, and more conservation and restoration. We need many more people to combine their awareness with behavioral modification, community organizing, and political processes to turn this around. It's not clear at this point whether we will avoid the collapse of Earth's systems and, ultimately, human civilization. If we are to avoid such utter disaster, we must transform the way we think, behave, and treat one another and life on this planet. Both inner and outer transformations are required. Birds help with our awareness so we can better work to change human social, political, and economic systems, and collectively resist the lure of domination and oppression. Birds are a gateway to recognizing injustice, and their calls motivate necessary transformations.

Bird Bathing

The act of birding invites you into a world with more belonging, beauty, connection (to other humans, species, self, and life), community, wonder, awe, resilience, joy, mindfulness, presence, entertainment, caring, health, scientific understanding, gratitude, integration, and flow.[7-23] This book will guide you to increase not just the number of your encounters, but the quality and impact of them. The accidental encounter with a hummingbird hovering within inches of you, a swan flying overhead, or a hawk swooping after prey in your backyard imbues your world with peace and awe. With training and intention, you can experience such wonders every day, throughout the day.

It is a practice to put yourself in the presence of birds and to open your awareness to them. The Japanese practice known as *shinrin-yoku*, or forest bathing, involves contacting with and taking in the atmosphere of a forest so that the nurturing aspects of nature cleanse and heal.[18] Bird bathing similarly utilizes wildlife within its biotic community, which may include a forest.

The Flock Needs You and You Need the Flock

Here's the wonderful thing about birding: you don't have to be good at identification to get something out of it. Just the act of walking, looking up, focusing the mind on another being, and learning more about life around you are enough to reap immense benefits. As more people improve their own lives and the lives of birds, the biotic community is enhanced. That includes us. The more people connect to nature and grow more resilient and knowledgeable, the stronger we all are.

We "bird" not just for ourselves, but for the whole world. Attuning ourselves to birds and their needs, we can move through life doing the least harm and helping birds live the life they freely choose when they are able. When birds have ultimate freedom, so do we. This lifelong practice will constantly challenge, grow, and reward you. It will rewire your brain to live in beauty, hold close tragedy, and reduce harm where you can, with both yourself and others.

Birds of a Feather — Even Those Without Feathers — Flock Together

Even if the definition of birding is limited to "the identification and observation of wild birds in their natural habitat as a recreation," birdwatching would include some 45 million people in the USA alone.[24] If we include appreciating, focusing on, caring for, and learning about birds, the numbers are much greater. They then include those who say they love birds, have bird art, have homed a bird, watch bird documentaries, read bird poetry, swerve their car to get a better look when an unusual bird flies overhead, or brake when one crosses in front of the car. Over 57 million United States households maintain bird feeders in their yards, spending more than $4 billion annually on bird food.[25] There are also numerous organizations with professionals concentrating on birds, including veterinary clinics, bird clubs, nonprofits, parks, reserves, universities, and government agencies. That's a lot of people thinking about and benefiting from birds, who in turn could be a resource for care and conservation actions directed towards wildlife.[26]

This Guide as Your Flight Simulator

Young growing birds of some species need long periods to perfect their flying. They often stay in trees or on the ground until they are ready to fly. Birds that have been rescued often need time to heal and must have flight training before they can be released into their natural habitats. So too for us, it's going to take some time to heal and learn better ways to live well together. We don't really know what that looks like yet. Not all birds can soar or run after being harmed, but they can be cared for and loved. This book is ultimately about love, and the freedom and joy that comes from a life centered around empathy, connection, reality, and science.

Maybe right now we can't see how to form a more flourishing society, but we can learn to flow in the moment and catch glimpses of what freedom looks like. As a youth in the Civil Air Patrol, I trained on flight simulators. They were cramped and clunky devices in those days, not resembling actual flight through the clouds in a plane. To learn to fly, you actually have to fly. But you have to learn the basics first.

Here I present some basic guidelines and theory, but not too much, since I want you to get outside so birds can teach and grow you. I have compressed the chapters, with each chapter followed by corresponding practices. The practices also contain more theory and explanation, so I invite you to read the practices, even if you don't undertake them. I don't want to tell you how to be with birds because, hey, I'm still learning myself. This is a "green book" that can grow as readers let me know what they need and what they learn. Though I am no Walt Whitman, I admire his approach to publishing successive editions of *Leaves of Grass* over the years. For this reason, this book is under a Creative Commons license, because together we are creating ways to heal ourselves and our Earth. Income and donations from distributing this book will support bird conservation.

The guide follows the structure of One Earth Conservation's Nurture Nature Program. One Earth Conservation is a nonprofit organization founded by Gail Koelln and myself, and features within our Nurture Nature Program our Birding for Life Walks. They are based on five human intelligences: emotional, social, multispecies, ecological, and spiritual. Each of these overlapping intelligences is necessary for an overall acceptance of reality and compassionate response to the beauty that connects us all. That said, feel free to skip around in the book to the areas you most need at any time. Please do, however, consider each intelligence. We need them all.

The central part of the book provides ideas, exercises, and theories for engaging with multispecies intelligence with our emphasis on birds. The final chapters guide the reader in intersectional justice practices that address core oppressions and aim for co-liberation. The book concludes as it began, urging you to become as perfect a birder as you can, not by having the longest "life list" of birds seen, but by having the longest list of lives saved (including, perhaps, your own). You will be immersed in beauty and will grasp that beauty never leaves you, because it lives in you.

Now put the book down, go outside, and be with birds. Play with them. They will teach you well.

Notes

1. MacLellan L. New data show that birding mania isn't just a lockdown fad. *Quartz*. Last modified June 25, 2021. https://qz.com/2024279/birdings-popularity-is-lasting-beyond-the-pandemic
2. State of the World's Birds: Taking the Pulse of the Planet (2018). *BirdLife International.* https://www.birdlife.org/papers-reports/state-of-the-worlds-birds
3. Gyllenhaal A, Gyllenhaal B. Vanishing by the Billions. A *Wing and a Prayer: The Race to Save Our Vanishing Birds*. Simon and Schuster; New York, NY. 2023.
4. Nature's Dangerous Decline 'Unprecedented' Species Extinction Rates 'Accelerating.' *Intergovernmental Science-Policy Platform on Biodiversity and Ecosystem Services* (IPBES). 2019. https://www.unep.org/news-and-stories/press-release/natures-dangerous-decline-unprecedented-species-extinction-rates
5. The State of the Birds, United States of America 2022. *North American Bird Conservation Initiative.* https://www.stateofthebirds.org/2022/
6. Rosenberg K, Dokter A, Blancher P, et al. Decline of the North American avifauna. *Science* 366(6461). 2019. https://www.science.org/doi/10.1126/science.aaw1313
7. Buxton RT, Pearson AL, Lin HY, et al. Exploring the relationship between bird diversity and anxiety and mood hospitalization rates. *Geo: Geography and Environment* 10:2023. https://rgs-ibg.onlinelibrary.wiley.com/doi/full/10.1002/geo2.127
8. Cox DT, Shanahan DF, Hudson HL, et al. Doses of Neighborhood Nature: The Benefits for Mental Health of Living with Nature. *BioScience* 67(2): 2017. https://doi.org/10.1093/biosci/biw173
9. Curtin, S. Wildlife tourism: The intangible, psychological benefits of human-wildlife encounters. *Current Issues in Tourism* 12: 2009:12. Last modified December 1, 2010. https://www.tandfonline.com/doi/abs/10.1080/13683500903042857

10. Fisher JC, Bicknell JE, Irvine KN, et al. Bird diversity and psychological wellbeing: A comparison of green and coast blue space in a neotropical city. *Science of the Total Environment* 793: 2021. https://www.sciencedirect.com/science/article/pii/S0048969721037256
11. Hammoud R, Tognin S, Burgess L, et al. Smartphone-based ecological momentary assessment reveals mental health benefits of birdlife. *Scientific Reports* 12:2022. https://doi.org/10.1038/s41598-022-20207-6
12. Haupt A. Birdwatching has big mental-health benefits. Here's how to start. *Time Magazine* November 14: 2022.
13. Hepburn L, Smith A, Zelenski J, et al. Bird Diversity Unconsciously Increases People's Satisfaction with Where They Live. *Land* 10(2): 2021.
14. Louv R. *Our Wild Calling: How Connecting with Animals Can Transform Our Lives – and Save Theirs.* Chapel Hill, NC: Algonquin Books. 2019.
15. Methorst J, Rehdanz K, Mueller T, et al. The importance of species diversity for human wellbeing in Europe. *Ecological Economics* 181: 2020. https://doi.org/10.1016/j.ecolecon.2020.106917. Accessed February 13, 2024
16. Stobbe E, Sundermann J, Ascone L, et al. Birdsongs alleviate anxiety and paranoia in healthy participants. *Sci Rep* 12. 2022. https://doi.org/10.1038/s41598-022-20841-0
17. Pizer, A. *The psychological benefits of wildlife viewing – Where isthewildlife.com.* Last modified December 17, 2015. https://www.linkedin.com/pulse/psychological-benefits-wildlife-viewing-andy-pizer
18. Sherwood H. Getting back to nature: how forest bathing can make us feel better. *The Guardian.* Last modified June 8, 2019. https://www.theguardian.com/environment/2019/jun/08/forest-bathing-japanese-practice-in-west-wellbeing
19. Strassmann, JE. *Slow Birding: The Art and Science of Enjoying the Birds in Your Own Backyard.* Tarcher Perigee: Los Angeles, CA. 2022.

20. Wildlife watching and tourism: A study on the benefits and risks of a fast growing tourism activity and its impacts on species. *United Nations Environment Programme (UNEP) and the Secretariat of the Convention on the Conservation of Migratory Species of Wild Animals (CMS)*: 2006. https://www.cms.int/sites/default/files/document/ScC14_Inf_08_Wildlife_Watching_E_0.pdf. Accessed on February 13, 2024
21. Watts, T. *Keep Looking Up: Your Guide to the Powerful Healing of Birdwatching.* Hay House Inc: New York, NY. 2023
22. Weir K. Nurtured by nature: Psychological research is advancing our understanding of how time in nature can improve our mental health and sharpen our cognition. *Monitor on Psychology* 51(3): 2020. https://www.apa.org/monitor/2020/04/nurtured-nature
23. Xu W, Zheng D, Huang, P, et al. Does Bird Diversity Affect Public Mental Health in Urban Mountain Parks? – A Case Study in Fuzhou City, China. *International Journal of Environmental Research and Public Health* 19: 2022. https://doi.org/10.3390/ijerph19127029
24. 2016 National Survey of Fishing, Hunting, and Wildlife-Associated Recreation. U.S. Department of the Interior, U.S. Department of Commerce, Bureau USC. U.S. *Fish and Wildlife Service:* 2016. https://www.census.gov/content/dam/Census/library/publications/2018/demo/fhw16-nat.pdf
25. Birding in the United States: A Demographic and Economic Analysis. Report_2016_508. Addendum to the 2016 National Survey of Fishing, Hunting, and Wildlife-Associated Recreation Report 2016-2. *United States Fish & Wildlife Service.* https://digitalmedia.fws.gov/digital/collection/document/id/2252/rec/2
26. People who feed birds impact conservation. Virginia Tech. *Science Daily* Last modified March 26, 2019. https://www.sciencedaily.com/releases/2019/03/190326081337.htm

JOYNER

Nesting Intelligence
Introduction to Five Natural Intelligences

Build Your Nest and It Will Come

As a parrot conservationist, I have put up nest boxes in many countries because there aren't enough natural cavities for parrots' use. We take measurements of natural cavities and mimic them as best we can by building boxes with a variety of designs. It's a good conservation tool, although we never know who is going to see these nest boxes as a home and nest. My very first attempt at using nest boxes was in Guatemala in the 1990s. Nearly every box filled up with Africanized bees, and we became quite popular with local beekeepers, who took the colonies that weren't too aggressive for their apiaries and the honey. One wooden nest box contained bees so aggressive that they swarmed inside my car I had naively parked near the tree. Other times, mammals, reptiles, and other species of parrots housed themselves in the boxes as well.

Just because we build something, doesn't mean it will be used by the intended guest. However, build a nest box and something will come. Construct your intention, and your life will fill with something — just maybe not what your plotting ape-brain desired. But sometimes nest boxes are on target, and a species is saved. You and the Earth could be too.

But I Don't Know How to Build a Nest

Birds are hatched with an innate propensity to use what is in their environment for their nests. Many species of birds build nests using grass, hair, fur, paper, ribbon, feathers, moss, stones, cigarette butts, and — well, you get the idea. Anything they can get their beaks on. The foundation for mindful birding in my case is any and everything I was able to get my hands on over the years that made the most sense. What was available for me, and is for everyone, is our natural human intelligences that we can develop by using evolution's gifts.

In 1983, Howard Garner in his book, *Frames of Mind: The Theory of Multiple Intelligences*, proposed eight human intelligences and later added a ninth.[1]

- Logical-mathematical intelligence
- Linguistic intelligence
- Spatial intelligence
- Musical intelligence
- Bodily-kinesthetic intelligence
- Intrapersonal intelligence
- Interpersonal intelligence
- Naturalistic intelligence
- Existential/spiritual intelligence

We will highlight some of these, but in a different order and categorized somewhat differently. Intrapersonal intelligence and bodily-kinesthetic intelligence fall under "emotional intelligence," while interpersonal intelligence is divided into social intelligence (human) and multispecies intelligence. Naturalistic intelligence, which in some constructs includes other species, we call ecological intelligence. Existential intelligence, reframed here as spiritual intelligence, in many ways is a cumulation of the previous four. These are the five intelligences nurtured during observing birds, and they interconnect. As you read this book, it will become clear how these categories of intelligence are a human construct to help us design our birding practice (see Five Intelligences chart below).

FIVE INTELLIGENCES CHART

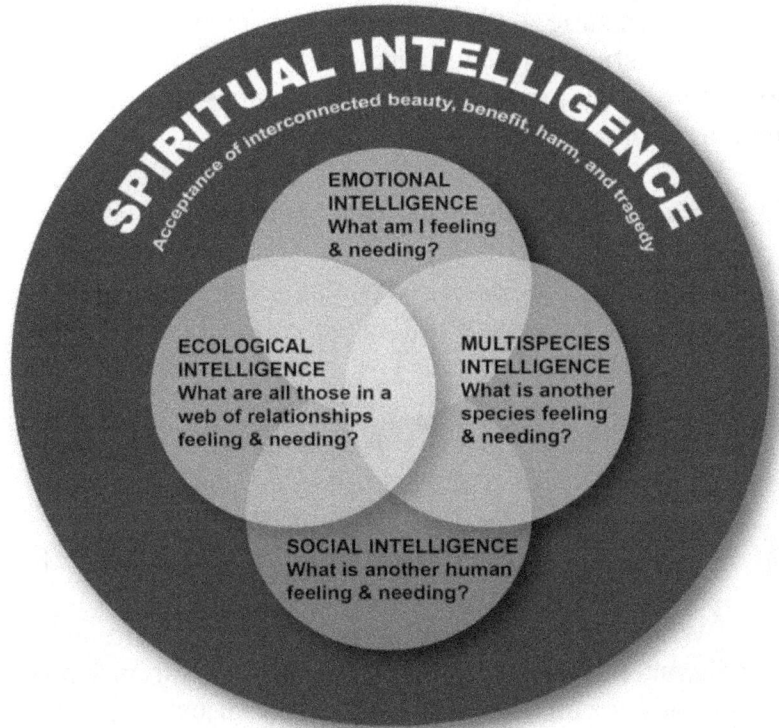

Though emotional intelligence (EI) and social intelligence (SI) seem far removed from birds with their human emphasis, they are imperative in a birding practice. For if we do not understand and accept ourselves, we cannot understand and accept others. However, bird mindfulness practitioners might choose to begin with the intelligences more directly related to birds — such as multispecies intelligence (MI) and ecological intelligence (EcI) — and explore the others at different times. Indeed, as the intelligences are all related and co-nurture one another, one can begin with any chapter or exercise in this book.

These intelligences, acquired from individual genetics and subsequent nurturing, can add not just to an individual's fulfillment but can also increase the overall health and potential of human units of organization. From friendships, families, and extended families to institutions, municipalities, regions, nations, and the global community, growing these intelligences contributes to both inner and outer transformation.

Where Was This Idea of Natural Intelligences Hatched?

The line separating good and evil passes not through states,
nor between classes, nor between political parties either
— but right through every human heart —
and through all human hearts.
This line shifts. Inside us, it oscillates with the years.
And even within hearts overwhelmed by evil, one small bridgehead
of good is retained.
– Aleksandr Solzhenitsyn, The Gulag Archipelago

While healing from my years of living in Guatemala during the civil war, I served congregations as a Unitarian Universalist minister and took an active part in local social justice efforts. While in El Paso, Texas, as part of my ministry I took to the streets to protest the build-up to the 2003 Iraq invasion by the USA. We banged drums and our heads against the wall to no avail. War came, as it did in Guatemala, and I had all I could take of what seemed like useless attempts to live in and build peace. I thought, "if I can't stop the violence in that way, maybe I can change the violence within me." I was learning that the line between the "good guys" and the "bad guys" doesn't lie between one group of people and another, but within every human heart.

I didn't know how to reduce the violence in my own heart and wiring, so I took to the internet in search of a better life — perhaps like you did to find this book. I discovered Nonviolent Communication (NVC), a system of thought with techniques and practices founded by the late Marshall Rosenberg.[2] Amazingly, he was offering a conference the next weekend in a nearby city, so I went. Walking into the room, I saw a man using animal puppets to hold conversations that expressed the tenets of NVC, which were intended to reduce judgment of the self and others in order to increase connection. When he set down the puppet, he sang his lecture. I admire a person with a good schtick, and he had several, though he had me with the puppets.

I thus began my serious training in this practice that informs my understanding of why and how to grow these five natural intelligences. Add a strong dash of science, cognitive ethology, and social science, and voilà, I slowly developed my own schtick over the years. Striving to become the most objective observers we can while watching how we judge and blame helps us foster connection, resilience, and, well, a bird's eye view of accepting reality.

Paradoxically, we strive to change the social constructs and behavior patterns that lead to harm even while growing our acceptance. Growing these natural intelligences through mindful birding is but one path to change. Heck, with serious intention, even reading the back of a cereal box could be used, but birds are a lot more interesting, as I hope you will also find this guide.

Emotional Intelligence
Loving Your Inner Bird

Love the world as yourself, and you will be able to care for it properly.

- Lao Tzu, The Tao Te Ching

Emotional Intelligence Is a Thing

There has been a lot of buzz about emotional intelligence over the last decades. Scores of books are at your disposal if you'd like to know more in terms of the theory and practice.[3-5] According to Peter Salovey and John Mayer, who first used the term EI, it consists of "the ability to perceive, evaluate and accurately express emotion; to access and/or generate feelings when they elude thought; to understand emotion and emotional knowledge, and regulate emotions to promote emotional and intellectual growth."[6] The word "emotion" broadly includes bodily states, affect (subconscious rapid emotional response), feelings, moods, and the catchall for many species, an internal subjective experience. Emotions are a common factor in many species, and humans have them for a reason: they are part of our neurophysiology that motivates us to move towards satisfaction and away from harm. Emotions are neither good nor bad, but rather exist as the feature of evolution that connects us to nature and to others. The greater awareness we have of emotions, the greater choice we have about our behavior that often is subconsciously directed by emotion. Even when we don't have a choice in the moment or even later, EI allows us to be present with emotions instead of pushing them away or judging others or ourselves for having them. Life is not about feeling comfortable but about feeling everything, and in that space we come completely alive, more whole and compassionate.

Emotional Intelligence Is a Good Thing

In the plethora of EI studies and books, various benefits are attributed to EI. It can improve our capacity for resilience, motivation, empathy, reasoning, stress management, communication, conflict management, and relationships with people and species. EI can also improve health by warding off depression, stress, and anxiety. One of the most beneficial emotions for our health that also leads to compassion for ourselves and others is empathy. Empathy for others and for ourselves are interconnected, facilitating and reinforcing each other. The beauty and needs that we deny ourselves we also deny to others, and what we deny to others we deny to ourselves. The more we see our own inner beauty, the more we reflect the beauty of others, bringing peace and possibility into the world. If we don't love and care for ourselves fiercely, we cannot be fierce advocates for this wondrous world and all beings within it.

EI brings to higher consciousness our emotions, feelings, moods, and bodily states. The limbic system, which is the location in our brains through which emotions communicate to our mind, body, and higher cognitive functions, is a slow learner. It takes repetition and practice to grow awareness of emotions and to manage them. If we can do this, we have greater choices regarding how to think, feel, and act. Nonviolent communication is not about getting it right or getting rid of uncomfortable emotions, but about increasing our choices. To be fully alive means feeling everything, the comfortable and uncomfortable. Don't push away any of it/ Whatever you're trying to ignore, deny, or suppress, that's what you're dead to. Life isn't about what you like. It's about what you open yourself to, attend to, learn from, and love.

The more honestly you see yourself for who you are without suppressing your feelings, the more tenderly honest you will be with others. You will more clearly communicate what you mean in a way that helps build connections and trust with others. This will help you be precise, open, and curious about communications with others and how they respond to you. If you suspect that your honest message will be painful, be ready to offer empathy to the receiver. Couple your honest messages with clear and doable requests in the moment.

For instance, you might be upset that your friend did not show up for an early morning birding activity. You are thinking that sure, five in the morning is early, but you made it! You could say that you desire respect and reliability and didn't feel that these needs were met in this situation You then call up your friend and first, before telling them how you feel about their "no show," you ask them what happened. You connect with their feelings and needs by guessing what might be going on for them. If you feel they have been heard, you can then share your disappointment that your desire for respect was not met because you had arranged your schedule so as to meet them and they did not show up. If your friend responds with something like, "We always have to arrange our meetings based on your schedule," you might choose to ask them what their feelings and needs are around this before moving to a request or further sharing of your own internal states.

Being honest with others helps us to live authentically and be more deeply connected to life, no matter how the other people around us react. Honesty, authenticity, and connection communicate acceptance of the self and others, which results in being heard and understood. Honesty and empathy give us tools to live better with ourselves and in our world, and to nurture our relationships and communications so that all have a greater chance to flourish. We need to be healthy and resilient humans who nurture all of nature, including birds.

Cut the Buzz and Tell Me What Is Happening

I have just used a lot of buzz words, so here is why this practice is important to me. I have heard from those explaining their Zen meditation practice as, "I do this practice because I am in the remedial group that most needs to work on this." This would be true of me and EI.

Nearly 25 years ago I began this practice of intentionally nurturing my natural intelligences because I was desperate. I was feeling life so strongly that I didn't know I had much choice in how to engage in life. Depression haunted my life, and coming back from living in Guatemala during the civil war with post-traumatic stress disorder made things ever so worse. Many healing components helped me regain the necessary balance to return to frontline conservation in Central America, including going to Divinity School, having a stable family life, and engaging in meaningful work. My hypothesis is that the work of EI within the framework of NVC, with its foundation of both emotional and social intelligence, was most impactful on improving my life satisfaction and contributing to others' as well.

What exactly is this practice of growing our natural EI? It is translating everything you think, say, or do into feelings and needs. It is to ask as a nonjudgmental observer, "What am I feeling and needing?" Our limbic system, the part of our brains that largely handles emotions, might have a good emotional memory, but it doesn't tell time very well. That means that when we have an emotional response, especially if it is sustained, we are reacting to events that may have occurred years ago. The body has a terrific memory that taps into emotional learning even if it doesn't have much to do with a current situation. Telling yourself in your mind, out loud, or in writing what you are now feeling and needing allows your mind to rewire to the current circumstances and find solutions or connections based in the present. By repeating this practice, we lay down stronger neural pathways to the part of our brain that interacts in the now, not in the past.

For example, my father often expressed anger and judgment towards me, and used corporal punishment in order to "correct" my behavior. That memory was seared deep into my body, and I am still emotionally triggered around domineering men or situations that smack of patriarchy (which is just about everything). However, by redirecting my reactions with men or anyone exhibiting patriarchal domination — including myself — to the present time, I can calm my limbic system's impulse to flight or fight and embody my current choice of how to respond to a situation.

Working with feelings and needs has been especially important in order to reframe my inner chatter (about judging myself and others) into being an observer. Thus, I free myself from a sense of separation from goodness, beauty, and life, and I am present to life's tragedy, harm, and suffering. I have become a stronger advocate for myself, others, and birds, even when faced with critical and domination-based voices, actions, and intentions.

Mirror, Mirror, on the Wall, Why Should I Care About You at All?

> *You are a manuscript of a divine letter.*
> *You are a mirror reflecting a noble face.*
> *This universe is not outside of you.*
> *Look inside yourself;*
> *everything that you want,*
> *you are already that.*
> *If you are irritated by every rub, how will your mirror be polished?*
> \- Rumi, The Spiritual Couplets of Rumi

When I was five, I begged my parents to give me a parakeet for my birthday. When we went to the Woolworth's Five and Dime to pick out which color bird I wanted, the salesperson said, "Don't forget the mirror. Budgies love mirrors." What they should have said was: don't forget to get at least one other budgie. Budgies need a flock. But we didn't know that then, and many captive avians had only a mirror for company when their humans were busy elsewhere.

We, too, can be trapped with mirrors if we think the world is just a reflection of our inner life. This is part of what this book is about, seeing the world as not about us but with wonder. Mirrors can imprison us if we buy into the negative messages of our societies, and such reflections confirm the worst about ourselves.

Do you trash talk yourself when you look in a mirror? I'll be honest: To avoid these thoughts, I can go days without looking in a mirror. I'd rather face the day with toothpaste on my face than listen to self-chatter that is blind to the beauty within and without.

There is another way. As in the poem by Rumi, we can commit to a practice that shifts the mirror and shines it until we reflect the beauty that connects each of us to all. Growing our EI enables us to do this.

Self-Empathy Is Not Whining

Self-empathy is the foundational skill of EI. It means being curious about, accepting, and even celebrating your feelings and needs. I watch participants' body language when we get to this part of a workshop. I can see how some tense up because they don't want to appear weak. They have been conditioned that in order to garner respect and acceptance and be worthy of love and connection, they can't be a whiny baby. Others in the workshop may smile and visibly relax as I describe self-empathy. They are relieved that finally the most important person in their lives is going to listen to them — themselves.

". The real wisdom and learning come from within each person. Deep down, we know what we want and need. We slow down for a chance to untangle the mess our culture and upbringing snared us into.

Paying attention to our bodies, feelings, and needs is anything but whining. Self-care is a great service to life, and it takes courage and work. Marshall Rosenberg described self-empathy as a "deep and compassionate awareness of one's own inner experience." It is also a deep and compassionate awareness of the life around us. Then when we look in the mirror, we see the world.

Who Can I Blame for My Lack of Self-Empathy?

> *Beyond our ideas of right-doing and wrong-doing,*
> *there is a field. I'll meet you there.*
> *When the soul lies down in that grass,*
> *the world is too full to talk about.*
> *Ideas, language, even the phrase "each other"*
> *doesn't make sense anymore.*
> – Rumi, The Mathnawi of Jalalu'ddin Rumi

Self-empathy means identifying and considering our feelings and needs without judgment, and this is no easy task. We have internalized messages and stories from society to keep us safe, to motivate our behavior, and to ensure we have love, respect, and connection. We often do this at the cost of loving, respecting, and connecting to ourselves. When we realize the wonderful life we could have had for all those years or could have given others, uncomfortable feelings can arise. I see this time and again from many of us who grew up in societies or families where blame, domination, judgment, and bullying were the methods that became the means to meet our needs. If our needs were not being met, it was surely the fault of someone else — someone fundamentally wrong, at least in some aspects of their being.

The tools we use to think about others are the same tools we use to think about ourselves: we see ourselves as flawed and lacking. Such negative judgments harm our wellbeing, sap our energy, divert us from our goals and dreams, decrease our happiness and effectiveness, and affect our health. We need to be as healthy as possible so that other beings may be as well. What can be healthy is to open ourselves to what we are feeling and needing, so we spend less time on blaming and more time on acceptance. Paradoxically, our actions change ourselves and the world around us. Don't blame on, but rise to the challenge and think "game on"!

But I'm Terrible at Games!

But the irony of affective empathy is that it requires being really good at listening to one's self. A person has to be able to identify his or her own feelings to notice how they are resonating with someone else's.

– Andrew Price[7]

We have a game in our household of tossing stuffed Angry Birds at one another. I am not sure of the exact moment it started, but I recall that the game began when we had a Honduran teenager who we fostered and became our son. There were days when the differences were just too great and one or more of us wanted to sulk, but there is nothing like throwing soft funny things at someone to snap us out of the tedium of our own judgmental thoughts. High laughter always ensued, so much so that my abdomen would ache.

We carried that tradition, and the soft plushy birds, into our next household where various people came to live over the years. If at first it startled them to have something bonk them on the head, they soon learned to guffaw and throw plushies back with the best of them. I remember the expression of one toddler who tried to look indignant when she received her first soft hit (thrown by her father) and thought about crying. Then she looked at each of us laughing, and joined in. Now, whenever she comes to visit, she finds the pile of stuffed birds and entices us all into the game once more. The father of that child was a baseball pitcher and there is no competing with his aim, but then he'll get bonked with a sly toss from an unsuspecting and demure source – his spouse – who regularly claims she's not good at games or athleticism, but sure is good at having fun. No matter where we begin, we can make our lives into a light-hearted game as we develop our EI.

Our pursuit of growing our EI invites playfulness because of the very plastic nature of the human brain that constructs meaning and language to coincide with what our bodies communicate to us. According to the Constructive Emotion Theory, the entire brain constructs emotion with collaborating, multiple brain networks. There are no genetically hardwired emotions such as anger or joy. Instead, in any given moment, the brain predicts and categorizes the bodily affect via interoceptive predictions and emotional concepts produced from one's particular culture and experience in order to construct a physical experience of emotion.

The only thing that is truly biological is whether we are attracted or repulsed (level of pleasantness or unpleasantness) by something and if the arousal is low or high. The combination of valence (pleasant/unpleasant) and arousal (high/low) is our affect that tells our brain our body's energy status, and then the brain looks for an explanation for any unbalanced body energy state. Over time and much practice, it forms stories and words to describe the experience particular to each individual and modified by family and culture.

Just like a toddler learning to throw plush birds, a person's emotional intelligence is influenced by genetic predisposition and by encouragement (or discouragement) in the early years. However, almost all of us, whatever our genes or age, have the capacity to increase our emotional intelligence — at least a little bit — and develop our self-understanding and care. As animals, we know we have emotions, and we are almost constantly experiencing them. This doesn't mean we know we are having them, or which ones, especially if multiple responses to experience are occurring at the same time.

We have to bring to higher consciousness the emotions, feelings, moods, affect, and body states our mind and body are communicating, and approach the stories our brains create about our experiences with curiosity, uncertainty, and skepticism. It will take time to rewire our limbic system since this location in our brains through which emotions communicate to our mind, body, and higher cognitive functions is a slow learner. It takes repetition and practice to grow awareness of affect and the emotions we attribute to them and to manage them. If we can do this, we have greater choices regarding how to think, feel, and act.

What's Self-Empathy Got to Do with Birds?

For the last 3,000 words or so, we have not said much about birds, or any other species other than us great apes for that matter. I don't know about you, but for me that's way too long to concentrate on humans. I usually lose interest within a paragraph if what I'm reading references only mammals. The more EI and self-empathy you have, which translates to greater self-awareness, the more space you have to consider and be aware of the feelings and needs of birds, as well as all those with whom you are in relationship.

But wait, there's more! We share with most other species an inner subjective experience (feelings, emotions, body state, moods) that causes individuals to move toward satisfaction and benefit (needs) and away from harm and discomfort (needs). These are very basic definitions of feelings and needs that apply across life. The multispecies intelligence section of this book expands on this concept, but for now let's use these definitions to talk about humans. We are a species that uses language to shape not just our cultures but our very minds and bodies, and our minds in turn loop back to impact language.

When I talk about feelings and emotions, these words are filtered through the lens of my North American/European, white-skinned, cisgender, middle class, wanna-be-bird-but-great-ape female being. When I describe the bodily reaction I am experiencing as anger, this may not be the word or meaning that is used in another part of the world to describe the same reaction. In fact, some cultures might not even have a word for anger, and hence their bodies have a different reaction when, let's say, someone steals the food out of another's hand. There really are no universal feelings because language and culture shape the mind, and vice versa. We cannot say that certain feelings are universal, but the process of subjective experiences motivating our behavior is a mechanism that crosses species lines.

When we see that our bodies, including our brains, have a basic biology that connects us to other species, and when we are aware of how our thinking, behavior, and motivations have been heavily molded by experience and culture, two things happen. First, we feel a connection to birds because in many ways they are like us, and second, we are humbled as humans by how much sway culture has over our construction and interpretation of experience. In short, human brains are constructed by society. If we want to construct a reality based more on compassion, care, and equity, with mindful birding we can grow our EI, reconstruct our reality, and pass it on to the generations to come.

Now that we've really explored self-empathy, you might wonder if we can get back to exploring how to use words to describe our bodily state? Not quite yet!

Making Shit Up

We can use words to help describe what our bodies are experiencing, and to retrain our limbic systems to pay attention to what is happening now. But knowing that language and culture have shaped our minds and behaviors in profound ways that often don't make it into consciousness, it behooves us to seek new patterns of behavior by breaking out of the use of words whenever we can, or at least, to emphasize what is happening all over our body instead of just relying on conscious thought to change. There is no doubt a role for language and intentionality in mindfulness (hey, you reading this book is a good case in point), but because so many cultures overemphasize language, birding is our opportunity to break free of this lopsided mindset that "we are our thoughts." Scientists have learned that most behaviors and decisions come not from conscious thought, but from the body processing subjective experience (past and present) and reacting in certain ways, often before we are ever conscious of what we are doing.[8] In reality, we tell stories about why we did or do things in order to protect the ego, to stay safe, and to stay in community, but it may not be as close to reality and to experiencing wonder as we can get.

You Gotta Feel It in Your Fingers and Feel It in Your Toes

Our minds reside not just in our brains but throughout our bodies, which know stuff and are smart. If we want to be mindful, we must connect to what is going on in our bodies. This is why in birding we pay attention to bodies, ours and theirs, because bodies convey what is happening in ways that connect us across different cultures and species. How we describe feelings may not be universal, but the preciousness and needs of bodies are. By observing what our bodies are doing, we learn to name our bodies' intentions and perhaps change all that wiring that got crisscrossed generations before we were born. Immersed in the moment, we learn to understand our bodily states and the words we've been taught to describe them. I encourage everyone to experience birds without words so they can truly follow what human and bird bodies are doing, letting words go so we inhabit the whole body. There is a time for cognitive intent, and there is a time to just be. But there is always time to be aware that the possibility of beauty, connection, and love is actually all around us.

I learned this important facet to birding through my body and other bodies. I was leading a series of "Birding as Spiritual Practice" workshops at the Apache del Bosque Birding Festival in New Mexico and had set aside time for our congregation's children and families to join me for a half-day of birding. I led the children around a loop road, stopping every so often to look for birds and explain what we were seeing and feeling through various quotes, explanations, and exercises. I could tell I didn't really have the kids' attention, especially little Kenny who'd had a rough birth with a mother addicted to cocaine and lived with his grandparents. Kenny might not have been attentive, but the adults seemed unfocused as well. Trying to explain new concepts while beautiful birds and nature are all around often fails because people are distracted by the community nature experience.

We stopped at a pond full of white snow geese. The sun was perfectly situated to show off the blue sparkle on the water, contrasting spectacularly with the white of so many birds. I had a bird poem, "Wild Geese," by Mary Oliver I wanted to read that ends with this line:

> *Whoever you are, no matter how lonely,*
> *the world offers itself to your imagination,*
> *calls to you like the wild geese, harsh and exciting –*
> *over and over announcing your place*
> *in the family of things.*[9]

Before I could recite these words, the birds accomplished what I could not. Hundreds of white geese suddenly took to the air and flew over us. Their wings clapped like thunder, and their essence vibrated into our depths. Kenny jumped, squealed, danced, and then ran into his grandparents' arms. The other children did likewise until the clusters of small families fell into silence as birds streamed over our heads. Everyone was suddenly alive, focused, joyful. This was not the result of human cognition alone, but from being with birds and feeling them from our heads to our toes. Being with birds allows us to socially construct new words for our experiences, and for those words to develop our body's reactions in an ever-present feedback loop where language begins and ends in the body.

Maybe we need new words to describe the emotions evoked by nature's spontaneity, so that we can construct and share our compassionate experiences. What words can you think of to describe what you feel when you experience the wonder and beauty of birds? Birdiful? Awebird? Maybe we can use the names of the birds to instill language into our sense of wonder, connection, and community. When I go for walks and see a bird, I say, "Hi, starling!" or "Hello, blue jay!" When it comes seeing a flock of Canada geese, I just say, "Hi, geese," to interconnect them with the profound preciousness of everyone and Earth.

I'm Not Needy, I'm Wanty

When I give workshops that emphasize EI and self-empathy, I often get reactions such as these:

> "I was never given permission to think about my own needs. I was taught that's selfish. Now I see that it is self-ful. What a relief" (often said with wet eyes).

> "I don't want to be seen as 'needy.' Can't you use another word?"

A dear friend a few years ago gave me a kitchen magnet with a woman on it saying, "I'm not needy. I'm wanty." It adorns my refrigerator, reminding me that we humans often don't want to acknowledge that we have needs — and if we do, they might need to be subservient to the larger group. The magnet reminds me daily that individual needs are important, and that we also must tread carefully in order to pay attention to the needs of the group. The extremes of investing too much in only either the self or the community can lead to self-denial and other types of subjugation. This is especially true because we live among abusive people and societal systems which can cause disconnection from or lower compassion for others and ourselves. The needs of each of us are interrelated to the needs of each other and the whole. It's not a competition between self and others, but a synergy that holds precious the needs of every being and attends to finding ways to care for everyone. Needs don't compete; they synergize. Every individual needs to flourish if biotic and human communities are to flourish.

Needs by Any Other Name

> *Needs may not be universal, but they do matter.*
> – John Burton[10]

In the Nonviolent Communication (NVC) community, it is nearly a cardinal rule that our needs are described as universal. This can run afoul of the concept of multiculturalism in the same way that the concept of feelings does. The language of needs and the idea that we are all hardwired to have the same needs entangle with a dominant culture that prescribes what others feel and need. I do think that as biological beings we all share basic needs, such as safety, nutrition, water, and health, but what about the more complex needs such as friendship, meaning, and wealth? Like emotions, these needs are socially constructed and may not have any biological fingerprints. Yet there seem to be similarities across cultures. Research about universal human needs from a justice perspective resulted in various short lists that expand the basics to include societal needs (security, freedom, equality, and tolerance) and individual needs (identity, relatedness, security, and recognition).[10] I am cautious to impose these assumptions of universality on all human cultures, but still use them in my toolbox of connecting to others.

Even this abbreviated list of needs is complicated by our brains' wiring that is influenced by our experiences and cultures, as well as our genetic and physiological orientations. So how do we progress? Let's go back to the basics. What ties humans to other species? What are our most basic needs? Let's describe them as either those that bring comfort and benefit, or those that relieve or avoid discomfort and harm.

Researcher Lisa Barrett is even more fundamental in her definition of basic needs, that encompasses her constructed mind theory. She states that individuals strive to regulate their body state when it senses pleasantness or unpleasantness at various levels of arousal.[6] All beings have these basic needs. For all species, cultures, and individuals, their subsets of needs can be derived from the basic understanding of needs as previously defined.

This helps serve as a basis for us to understand what words individual brains use to describe needs based on individual bodily states. Every person may note the words they use and make a list of ideas and images in any given period of time. One can also start with a standard list (such as the Feelings and Needs List in the Appendix) and investigate which words resonate in any given situation. Often the body will self-regulate when a word is matched with a specific bodily state, suggesting that we can impact the body through language, even if the circumstances have not changed.

For instance, in workshops I ask people to consider their level of arousal or affect (high or low) and whether they are sensing their body is moving away from discomfort and harm (unpleasantness) or towards comfort and benefit (pleasantness). Each individual shares the words that describe their experience if that helps them to be more specific and communicate with others. We always go back to basic body experience to rewire ourselves around cultural constraints of what needs are and are not "allowed," or other stories we might be making up around our needs. This same approach extends to other humans (social intelligence) and other species (multispecies intelligence), both of which will be discussed later.

Sometimes our bodily state does not tell us what we need to be doing right now. We might be in a certain mood which impacts what we think we are experiencing, as well as what we think we and others must do. Our moods can impact our actions and thoughts in many ways. For instance, judges deliver harsher sentences right before lunch than after because hunger causes mood shifts.[11] Sometimes we might have a heated argument with a loved one because we didn't get enough sleep the night before. In general, we should be aware of how our moods can subconsciously lead to poor outcomes. I often tell people that if they are having sustained uncomfortable emotional reactions to circumstances to try to regulate their bodily state by taking a nap, eating a snack, drinking water, meditating, or stepping outside to look up (which has a calming effect).

I explained this once right before a lunch break during an NVC workshop. As we reconvened, a woman came up to me, gushing, "It works, "It works!" She had been taking a carful of children to McDonald's for lunch, and her young child was about to go into full-on tantrum mode in the back seat. She told me, "So instead of yelling at her or threatening punishment, I asked if she was hungry. Knowing that as a child she might not realize what her clearly aggrieved bodily state was telling her, I said we would be getting lunch soon. She immediately calmed for the rest of the ride to the restaurant."

Is Birding a Universal Need?

It can help people to think of challenges in terms of motivation, values, and desires. All of these can be used as tools to understand our inner world while digging deeper by asking, "What is the need under the need?" For example, let's imagine someone whose employer suddenly shifted their schedule so they cannot go to the park in the evening to watch birds. They might say to themselves, "I need to go birding!"

The creative exercise would be to see that birding doesn't fall under any of the categories normally constituted as a universal need (although this book argues it is, or at least it has been in my life). Though being with birds is prime in many lives, let's consider what the basic motivation behind birding is. The activity moves toward benefit and comfort, and perhaps moves away from harm and discomfort, depending on one's home and work life. There may be low arousal, such as the feeling of, "Drats, it would have been nice to get out this evening," or higher arousal, such as, "I cannot survive another minute if I don't see the migrating painted bunting on the rare bird alert." We could end the exercise here by simply stating that these examples are motivated to move towards or away from what is helpful or harmful, respectively. But let's dig deeper.

Why do you want to go looking for birds? It could be, such as in my case, for the enjoyment of beauty, company, connection, stimulation, and fun. These needs can be met by other activities, which helps us understand that birding is one strategy to meet deeper needs. When searching to recognize underlying needs, it is helpful to conduct a body scan. What is my body telling me if I suddenly cannot go watch birds?

I spend less time with wild birds when I am not in the field working on parrot conservation that involves many hours outdoors counting parrots and taking in all the other wildlife around me. Back at home, I am in front of a computer most of the day to get as much done as possible for the birds and people I serve: writing reports and grant proposals, and networking with others who can help our conservation efforts. Many needs are met in this indoor work, including meaning, purpose, and mattering — but let's face it, it's not birding. In this setting, my body has a low level of arousal that might be called depression. But if I go out birding with others, or return to one of my project sites, I find myself almost giddy. My body becomes animated, there is a smile on my face, and I laugh when a bird demonstrates almost any ordinary behavior in front of me. Like little Kenny, I want to run and jump. If I am with people, I search their eyes to connect and share. My body clearly tells me that I am moving towards benefit at a high level of energy.

With this insight, in order to grow one's EI, one must begin with an awareness of feelings and needs. This orientation allows us choices. I am dependent on birds and bird conservation work to meet many of my needs. If working with birds to improve their welfare is my primary strategy without many other options, my ability to regulate my body state, emotions, and needs is limited. Who wants to be depressed in front of a computer all day? Periodically, I remember my needs other than being with birds and develop strategies to meet these needs. Because I have such strong neuronal reactions to birds and I can trigger positive emotions just by imagining them or talking about them, it is difficult for me to find any other strategies that are quite as powerful.

I am not alone. Birdwatching can also boost positive emotions, which are a foundation for wellbeing. In one study, two groups counted birds, but one group also rated their joy upon seeing each bird species.[12] Both groups received boosts in wellbeing; however, the joyful group reported dramatic improvements. This indicates that being aware of positive emotions while birdwatching — that is, employing emotional intelligence — can boost benefits. Increasing the hours that one watches birds can further illicit a profound sense of tranquility.[13]

Being aware of birds doesn't just produce positive emotions. My parrot conservation work supports my need for beings to flourish, and this awareness of birds includes being aware of their suffering. For this reason, during my late thirties I moved away from bird activism because I could not take the constant reminder of loss. I needed more choices of how to meet my needs and regulate my bodily state and emotions. Developing my EI skills has added other ways to respond to the world with my toolbox, and has improved my resilience when deciding how to best serve others. Below are exercises that might do the same for you.

Birding and Emotional Intelligence Practices

For help in conducting these exercises, please use the Feelings and Needs List in the Appendix.

Practice 1: Birding Is Stretching Yourself

Moving our bodies into certain configurations impacts our emotional response to the world. It can shift our thinking, open us to connection, and offer a greater repertoire of choices and behaviors with which to meet the vicissitudes of daily living. For this reason, stretches and practices that involve the body are recommended before conducting any inner or outer work (such as birding and social change). Our bodies can lead us into greater awareness and connection to self, birds, other humans, and the entire biotic community. We begin our bird walks with the following body movements

1. Breathe deeply in, as much as you are able, and then do a long exhale. Do this as many times as comfortable, three if possible.
2. Open your arms to the side, as wide as you are comfortable doing. Breathe deeply as you do so.
3. Now raise your arms above your head and look up. See the sky, the clouds, the trees, and maybe the moon and stars.
4. Minding your balance, and if you are able, look up as you turn slowly around in place, in a full 360-degree turn. Do this slowly while breathing deeply.
5. Now place your hands together and bow to one another and the trees and to any other presence, such as rivers, mountains, etc.
6. If you able, continue the bow and touch the ground. Feel the grass, dirt, stones, and rocks.
7. If you are able to do so, sit on the ground. Ask others to help you get up if you aren't sure you can. Then lie on your back and breathe deeply. Stretch out your arms and take in the whole world. You can also roll onto your stomach and look deeply into the grass or plants around you. Breathe deeply and smell the life that is also you. When you are ready, return to a sitting or standing position.

How Stretching Helps Us Connect

1. Breathing deeply: This is suggested in a variety of mindfulness and therapeutic techniques and there is a reason for this. When we breathe deeply, we invite the body to relax. Short shallow breaths are a sign of tension or anxiety, but if the body breathes deeply, the expanding lungs press the vagus nerve, which is large and runs from our brains and throughout our abdomen. Stimulating the vagus nerve triggers the parasympathetic body response. This leads to slower respiration and heart rate, and lower blood pressure. The body relaxes and opens our whole being to what is happening right now instead of triggering

heightened responses of the sympathetic nervous system that communicates danger or discomfort. By breathing deeply, we can reduce stress, relax, and open ourselves to learning because our limbic system, which prompts the sympathetic response, isn't telling us to protect ourselves.

2. Opening the arms: To understand this body stretch, I ask people to demonstrate for me their body position when they are uncomfortable, tense, afraid, or even under attack. People lower themselves to the ground and move their shoulders and arms closer together to protect themselves. When we open our arms, we are signaling to our brain and body that we are safe, and that it is okay to be open with others around us — including the trees and the birds.

3. Looking up: Studies indicate that looking up can lead to greater kindness and compassion due to increased integration of the brain and body and opens space for us to connect to life around us. More will be said about the importance of looking up and its benefits in the Ecological Intelligence chapter.

4. Turning around: When we turn around, we are slightly off balance, and able easily to coordinate protective or fleeing actions. Once again, we are telling ourselves that everything must be okay if we are willing to be off balance. I have seen children's soccer games where the backfield players twirled and cartwheeled if the ball was far from them. It was as if they had to do something to connect to the joy and physicality of the game as part of the team, even if they couldn't get a foot on the ball.

5. Bowing: Many religions include bowing as part of their traditions. So do hierarchical social systems, such as curtseying and bowing before royalty. Can you think of other animal species that bow or get low? Various species of mammals, such as the dog or wolf, lower their front legs with their rear ends up when they are playing. They lie down or roll on their backs, showing their vulnerable necks and abdomens to others in play or submission. Similarly,

humans do somewhat the same. Bowing tells others that we are on their side with play, or perhaps in submission to their power. Bowing increases humbleness and compassion for others. In this way, our bodies once again leads the way for connecting us to others.

6. Touching the ground: Here we use our senses, including proprioception (perception of where our bodies are in space), to touch the ground, to put our bodies on the ground, and to smell. This moves us out of our conscious loops to absorb the world around us. Even if our brains are reluctant to stop inner thoughts replaying past experiences, our bodies and subconscious are connecting to the earth, which guides our conscious thoughts to do so as well.

Practice 2: Scanning Our Bodies While Scanning for Birds

We discussed how our bodies know much of what we need even if an exact need never surfaces into our consciousness. We are already jumping away from a snake on the ground before we are consciously aware that there is a snake. In such instances, our consciousness may not have much control. During one opening trout fishing season in the high mountains of California, I listened to the old-timers tell stories of times they had been afraid of rattlers. I thought they were wimps to be afraid of snakes. The next morning, I was hiking along a river where I was fly-fishing when my foot nearly came down on top of a rattlesnake. The snake's head and rattle came up. Before I knew what was happening, I had thrown my rod,, screamed, turned, and run away to my partner downstream. Still an arrogant young adult, I was slowly learning about the importance of body and mind. Just because I want to look tough by other's standards doesn't mean I can make it happen.

Several years later, I was in Brazil walking in the dark to a parrot count when a fer-de-lance, which is a large venomous pit viper, scooted across the trail in front of me. I shouted a warning to my colleague who managed to skip and hop, while the snake slithered between his feet that in flip flops. A bite would have threatened his life since we were a long distance from any hospital with antivenom. I was only a step behind him and didn't jump but instead stood still until the snake slithered away. I am not sure why. Perhaps it was my decades of thinking and learning about snakes and admiring them that balanced my reaction while still able to shout a warning. Maybe being sleepy or giving my attention to not falling over in the dark helped me not overreact. Whatever the cause I did not experience much anxiety or fear.

I have found this true of many other bodily reactions, such as my reaction to spiders and to certain social situations that used to trigger me more than they do now. My awareness of what my body does and the experience to reframe that as curiosity about my feelings and needs have helped me to develop more bodily regulation. I don't want to completely keep my body from jumping away from snakes, but with enough awareness I can remain connected to my surroundings, so I'm not skipping over any pleasurable and important experiences or buffering responsive actions. Sometimes I think a stick is a snake, and I don't want to waste energy or opportunities to help others because I don't have full awareness of my bodily state and my emotional construction of fear.

Engaging in adventures and the unknown can be part of the process of immersing ourselves in a more just and flourishing way of being in the world, and our body intelligence[14] can keep us as safe as possible. "Don't do anything stupid," was a mantra taught to me by my father. He first gave me this advice after I had just graduated from college and was about to spend the summer touring America, camping, and visiting friends and family in a Ford Pinto. It was a meaningful moment when my father hugged me and looked me in the eye. I thought he was going to share some deep wisdom as I was on the cusp of a great journey, but instead he spoke to me as if I were an irresponsible teen again. However, he gave the perfect advice. I have integrated his words into many situations, and his advice has meshed with my awareness of my bodily state and emotional constructs. I seem able to take risks without jumping into a pit of vipers.

Instances such as with the snake demonstrate that with practice, we can increase our communication to various parts of our body to increase choice and acceptance. One way to practice this is to conduct a body scan by taking the time to ask, "What is my body telling me now? What am I experiencing in various regions of my body?" There are two levels to a body scan practice: One is to simply experience the sensations in the body without words, and the other is to assign language to your experience.

Some of us have a more natural ability to know what is going on in our bodies, but we can all increase this capacity through practice. Remember that one tip for growing awareness is to slow down and take your time. Time for a body scan can happen during a bird walk and also before heading out, which allows you even more time to practice. On YouTube, various videos can guide you through body scan meditations, some in 10 minutes or more.

Body scans often follow a certain order, such as starting with the head and then checking in with various areas of the body and ending in the toes. Breathing deep and relaxing the body are suggested, and perhaps even closing your eyes (but not while walking!). As you move through various parts of the body you may ask yourself, "What am I sensing?" If you find yourself judging or telling stories about any sensations, take a breath and return to the sensation alone. For instance, you may find yourself frowning, and then realize your internal story may be, "I shouldn't be frowning. Others might see me." Or you might experience hunger and ask, "Why am I hungry now? I just ate. I've been eating too much lately." If you take a deep breath, you may release such judgments. Perhaps it will help if you simply say to yourself that you are hungry or that it's curious that you're frowning. Moving from judgment to curiosity helps grow your connection with and acceptance of your entire self.

This practice can be an intentional part of your birding experience, especially before you begin. You can not only grow awareness of your body, but you can also invite it to relax or stretch in various ways that increase the ability to connect. During a walk, you can periodically ask yourself what your bodily perceptions are and focus on birds to maintain mindful awareness in the moment. For instance, if you see an unusual species — perhaps a new or a rare one — check in with your body. Perhaps you are feeling somewhat tense as you want to make certain of your identification. You may start reminding yourself to take the requisite photos so no one thinks you are not a good birder. If you find yourself having thoughts like that or a shift in your bodily affect, take note of what your body is feeling. Are you tense? Perhaps you're holding the binoculars tighter than usual, breathing shallowly, or scrunching your facial muscles. Do you feel lighter? Are you still or moving? Perhaps these bodily responses would lead you to asking yourself if you are anxious, joyful, in awe, bored? Take the time to ask yourself these kinds of questions in many scenarios that may arise when watching birds:

- Do you see a bird chasing or attacking another? *You could ask yourself if you feel tension, aversion, or disgust.*
- Do you see a bird eating or drinking? *Does this suggest that you would like to drink or eat?*
- Do you see a bird that is sick or dead? *What is going on inside your body when you see this? What emotional words do you ascribe to this bodily state?*
- Do you see bird droppings under a roost tree? *Do you feel disgust? Curiosity?*
- Do you see a bird flying high? *Do you feel light, as if you had wings?*
- Do you see birds feeding their chicks? *Do you feel a softening, an urge to care and protect?*
- Do you see birds of different species looking for food? *Do you feel awe? Wonder? A sense of companionship?*

These exercises might seem mechanical at first, but a time will come when you automatically check in with your body around birds. Birds will begin to serve as a trigger for mindfulness through body intelligence and awareness, as well as self-empathy. Such awareness opens yourself to not just your own life, but to the lives of others.

Practice 3: Body Birding

Studies have shown that if we smile consciously, we can trigger feelings of happiness, though this may not be true in cultures where smiling denotes different emotions or meanings.[15] A smile causes a chemical reaction in the brain, releasing dopamine and serotonin. Dopamine increases feelings of happiness, and serotonin is associated with reduced stress. The less serotonin we have, the more depression and aggression we experience, and lower levels of dopamine are also associated with depression.

Patients who had Botox injections were not able to understand angry sentences as well as sentences that signified other emotions because they could not frown, and so their conscious selves didn't know how to interpret the written word.[15] One conclusion of this study of popular cultures is that when patients did not frown, the world seemed less angry and sad. In popular cultures, we hear aphorisms such as "Fake it until you make it," and "Smile and the whole world smiles with you."

Whatever your culture, you can move your face and body in order to stimulate a change in your emotions and bodily states. When I suggest this practice during a bird walk there are always a variety of responses based on individuality and culture, and each participant should experiment with what works for them. Besides consciously smiling and refraining from tense facial expressions, consider laughing. The short-term benefits of laughter include increasing your intake of oxygen-rich air, stimulating the heart, lungs and muscles, and releasing more endorphins from the pituitary gland. These molecules can reduce perception of pain and elicit feelings of euphoria. Laughter soothes tension and relieves stress responses. Long-term laughter improves immune functioning, increases feelings of happiness, and improves mood by warding off depression and anxiety.

Laughing during a bird walk also has social benefits. It helps people connect to one another and improves communication, bonding, agreement, affection, and emotional regulation. Like other facial and bodily expressions — but perhaps more than most — laughter is contagious. The brain responds to the sound of laughter and preps our facial muscles to join in the mirth.

Because laughter and humor are so good for individuals and groups, I encourage bird jokes or puns during walks. There are usually some groans in response but overall, any attempt to get people chuckling or smiling is good for our emotional and social wellbeing. I'll often walk with a list of puns and jokes related to the species we are likely to see. For instance, if we are near water, I'll explain why laughter is good for us, and that I want to quack people up. If we see or talk of owls, I'll explain the social implications of sharing the sighting so we don't feel owl by ourselves. Do you get the idea, or shall I go on? Do I hear a grown? I have placed a number of other bird puns throughout the book. How many can you find?

Another way to lead with the body is to purposely shift your body as you did during the stretches. For instance, you can walk with your shoulders back and your back straight, or add a spring to your step (safely of course), in order to invite connection and openness. When you see a bird, even a common one, exaggerate your facial expressions of joy and awe so that your whole self hears the herald to connect to the beauty around you.

Our bodies can bring us to the present moment and make connection as we slow down to register the sensations of taste, touch, smell, seeing, hearing, and proprioception. We can purposely invite the engagement of our senses by being silent during our birding outing. During this time, I ask people to just listen – to the wind, the leaves, the bird calls. I suggest they reach out and touch a plant or the ground, or hug a tree, being careful of poison oak or ivy. Our senses of touch and proprioception may lead us to think we are touched, which is why hugging a tree feels like we are hugged in return.

I also invite touch by bringing along taxidermized birds so that people can touch their feathers, beaks, and claws. I encourage people to pick up feathers along the way. Go ahead and smell a leaf or flower, but always check for bees and spiders first. Tasting is trickier as ground plants might have an undesirable residue, so I leave this step up to the discretion of others. Instead, I suggest that people lick their lips and taste the saltiness in the air or on their bodies. Using vision is natural for the sighted during bird watching, though sometimes we frown because we are trying hard to focus and concentrate. For this reason, I invite people to relax their faces and soften their vision, so they aren't focusing on anything near or far but taking in everything softly.

If you are leading a birding experience, it is important to remember that people have natural and acquired differences in their senses. Some see or hear better than others, and some have limited to no vision. I have led nature walks where people have nearly no vision, and I invite them to tell us what they sense. They often lead the rest of us in hearing and touching as the wind wraps us and our imaginations together.

Practice 4: Developing Awareness and Self-Empathy as if You Had Wings

> *Fully instantiated, care includes cognitive, affective, and behavioral components. In order to care ... people must be informed, people must feel, and people should act in ways that will express both their knowledge and their emotions.*
> – Susan Clayton and Gene Myers in *Conservation Psychology*[16]

We need a free flow of emotions and awareness of them for optimal mind and body integration, and wellbeing. Pushing away or being unaware of our own emotions makes it more challenging to accept and resonate with the feelings and needs of others. If we deny needs in ourselves, we deny them in others. If one of our daily mantras is, "I am too needy and should just pull myself up by my bootstraps," then we are prone to say that of others — such as thinking that birds can fend for themselves, are not suffering at all, or that we are more important than they are. In particular, if we don't acknowledge our own feelings and needs around bird issues and events, then we will move away from being present with birds and able to respond to their status with empathy. We can also do this with people, especially those we judge, categorize, and deem as "other." We may indeed use motivational talks to get ourselves to accomplish tasks or change our behavioral patterns to serve life ever more effectively, or seek to hold our species as a whole and as individuals more accountable. If we do, however, there are ways to do so without repeating restrictive or harmful societal messages.

First and foremost, we can use birds to strengthen the pathways for our conscious awareness of emotions. When you see a bird that strikes you with awe and wonder, take a moment to name the bodily state and emotional response with a quick body scan, much as suggested in Practice 4. Perhaps you feel joy, pleasure, appreciation, or curiosity when you see a new or unusual bird, or one that you particularly enjoy. Let's now add to Practice 4 by saying to ourselves, "When I see (insert bird description), I feel (insert emotion) because I need (insert need)." Undertaking such a practice will help you feel this emotion when you next see the bird. Maybe the response won't be immediate — and, indeed, brain rewiring is a lifetime practice — but over time you will experience more and more positive and pleasurable emotions when seeing a bird, any bird.

I was out watching birds one day with my spouse, who in our early days together didn't know much about birds, and he asked, "What is that species?" I said, "It's just a crow." He challenged me by asking, "What do you mean it's just a crow? Isn't this bird just as special as a snowy owl or a parrot?" He may have known more about birds than I do, at least in that moment. I had lost track of the wonder possible in every moment and every bird. Instead, I mimicked our culture's disdain for a species, which thankfully is changing. Ever since, I watch myself when I look at common birds, those who have been given a bum rap: crows, starlings, pigeons, English house sparrows, gulls, etc. With practice, being around birds will elicit a subconscious response, making joy and wonder a possibility even in the most urban or degraded environments where pigeons and sparrows offer delight. They are always wondrous, but we have to tend to our minds as humans are in a constant state of forgetfulness. For this reason, we practice or seek guidance from those who can help us — such as starlings, or Mary Oliver, who wrote of them in her poem, "Starlings in Winter."

> *Chunky and noisy,*
> *but with stars in their black feathers...*
> *Ah, world, what lessons you prepare for us . . .*
> *I want to be improbable beautiful and afraid of nothing,*
> *as though I had wings.*

Practice 5: Awareness and Acceptance of Uncomfortable Feelings

There are many bodily states and emotions that we can become more aware of, including uncomfortable feelings. With birds, as with all lives — including our own — this means understanding our own feelings of loss and mourning. Death is an ever-present companion of life, and pushing away any discomfort we have about death and suffering diminishes our capacity to respond to life, to nurture and be nurtured.

One day, I was out for a short stroll along our sandy road in Florida when I heard raucous bird calls approaching. I froze and looked all around as if the apocalypse was upon me. A Cooper's hawk flew right in front of me with a screaming, red-bellied woodpecker in her talons. Close behind the Cooper's hawk was a red-tailed hawk trying to take the catch for his own. Behind both hawks was a mixed species flock of smaller songbirds calling loudly, perhaps in a form of mobbing behavior. I still hear the woodpecker's cries and imagine myself in such a situation, and I shudder.

This episode showed me how a flock is beauty, tragedy, pain, suffering, and connection. To be present in such a moment and to have a choice, I need to recognize my reactive feelings and understand the needs of myself and others. Perhaps you too have had an experience such as witnessing a bird hit by a car, a baby bird fallen from a nest and injured, a cat with a bird in its mouth, or our increasingly silent and monotone landscapes as birds disappear from our lives. I cannot walk in the woods without thinking of the loss of our very own parrot in North America, the Carolina parakeet. They have been extinct for a hundred years but once flew from Nebraska to New York to Florida. An unknown author wrote, "My grandfather worked with the remaining flocks of Carolina parakeets. I mourn."

As you watch and learn about birds, on days when you are able, or with human company, allow yourself to mourn and name what is going on for you. Say or write to yourself: I am feeling (insert an emotion, such as sadness) because I need (insert a need, such as the wellbeing of birds). Remember that the needs of another being are related to your needs. The Carolina parakeet had a need for wellbeing, and we are left with a need for them.

Practice 6: Meet Needs When Needs Are Not Met

Being aware of our feelings and needs is the first step in having a choice about how we feel, and a choice about how to respond to those feelings. We can never bring back a bird that has died or an extinct species. Well, maybe we can with today's genetic technology, but they won't be the same species, as they will have different DNA and cultural learnings. Once a culture is gone, it is gone, and how to live in this world must be retaught to succeeding generations. There is so much that we cannot do, at least immediately, to alter the situation of birds and bring health to individuals and populations.

One response is to say we feel despair, depression, or anger, or a combination of any of these three and more, because the situation cannot be changed. Another response, using emotional intelligence, is to acknowledge those feelings and unmet needs and connect with what it feels like to have those needs met. This exercise can positively shift our resilience and connection to life instead of staying closed off to life in a defensive mode.

For instance, I can walk in the woods in the eastern United States and repeat to myself, "The Carolina parakeet is gone. What jerks humans are!" I have done this for decades. Then as I walk, I find myself frowning, I feel my jumpy and tight stomach, and I notice my shoulders are hunched forward. I am in a self-protective mode as I repeat this incantation of despair and doom.

If I shift this negativity by transforming it into a statement of feelings and needs, my body and thinking shift. For instance, when I am in the woods perhaps my need for beauty is being met, or I imagine how much I value the need for the wellbeing of all. Now I repeat to myself, "I love it when my needs are met for beauty and the wellbeing of other species." I find myself smiling, and my mood lightens. My stomach settles down, and my breathing deepens as my shoulders roll back. I have not changed the outcome; the Carolina parakeet is still extinct. However, I have connected to my own feelings and needs and honored those of others. This connects me to life. I experience more strength and courage to continue the crusade to keep future parrots from becoming extinct.

Try this yourself, not just once but frequently, daily, especially when you are around birds and telling yourself or others stories. Translate these stories into statements of feelings and needs, and see how your body shifts and new possibilities open for you.

Practice 7: Empowerment Through Self-Empathy

Building on Practice 6, we go a step further with reframing our thoughts and rewiring our minds. We do this by taking responsibility for our feelings so that we can do constructive inner work in the future and the present. This is not to say that when bad things happen other people or species do not cause them, or that it is not a natural human response to feel anger, sadness, or hurt. People who cause harm need to be held accountable, and it may serve an individual's purpose to use blame language such as, "You made me angry!" The invitation here, though, is to see if shifting some of your inner language opens up more choice, connection, and opportunity to meet needs for the most possible individuals and species.

This exercise begins with self-empathy. Write or say aloud, or even simply think of, the following sentence after doing a body scan and check what your body is experiencing now and how it might relate to current needs. "No wonder I feel (insert emotion). I really need (insert need)." This helps us connect to our needs and value them. You can journal this before you begin to birdwatch or find a restful place to write. You can also do this as you walk or move along a route. Breathe deeply before and after the first and second parts of this exercise and do your body stretches.

The second part of the exercise then ends with filling in the same feelings and needs into this sentence: "I am responsible for feeling (insert emotion) because I need (insert need)." This sentence empowers us and moves us from victimhood and judgment to choices. Consider any actions or needs that come up throughout this exercise that you would ask of others or yourself.

It is perhaps best to start off with a situation in which your body experiences comfort or benefits you as you ease into the practice. As you progress, you may wish to grow your self-empathy practice by choosing a situation in which you have experienced mildly uncomfortable feelings, and judged yourself or others to be unworthy or bad. To further challenge yourself, once you are ready, choose situations that were highly stressful or when you considered someone to be your enemy.

For instance, when you see a bird, ask yourself what your body is doing and what feelings arise. You might say, "When I see that woodpecker chick begging for food, I feel joy because I need the chick to be well and flourish." (Stimulation, beauty, and awe are the strategies for meeting the need of wellbeing.) You might even find yourself drawn closer to the parents feeding the chick because you desire to connect and share in the experience with others. You could also say that you have feelings of anxiety and concern because you desire for the newly fledged chick to be healthy and safe. The second part of the exercise then would prompt you to say, "I am responsible for my feelings of joy (or anxiety) because of my need for personal and avian wellbeing." As you say this, consider moving your body differently than you were before. Open up your arms, step lightly, and perhaps smile. All of this can shift your immediate connection to the self and to birds, and perhaps even cause a longer-term impact.

In my life, this has been of the utmost importance to me when I work in wild parrot conservation. I witness to so many sick and dying parrots due to poaching and trapping fueled by the wildlife trade, and I treat wild parrots harmed by wildfires, storms, illness, malnutrition, parasites, and predators. Intense feelings arise, and they can be exhausting, or alternatively I can disconnect from life around me and imagine that I have few options of what to do.

I have learned that even in times of violent human interactions or natural tragedies, I have more staying power than before to care for myself and others, and more choices of how to apply that care. Practicing inner work has kept me engaged in conservation in challenging geographic areas and situations that appear hopeless and dangerous.

Practice 8: Options Besides Birds in the Bush

Practice 8 is designed for when you can't get outside with birds, or perhaps being with birds isn't working out for you as you'd like. Follow the directions for Practice 7 and consider the following adaptions. First, you can substitute any species, including humans, for birds in this exercise. This would improve your life not just emotionally but also socially. Choosing other species also improves your multispecies intelligence. Many different species can be your gateway to wonder and can grow your sense of belonging in this world.

Though the effect might not be as pronounced when watching birds in videos or pictures, studies show that people still experience a positive impact from interacting with nature through media. Watching live webcams gives you the best chance to experience birds even if you can't be with them. (To find some, search for "bird webcams" on google or go to the Cornell University or Audubon websites.) You can also watch nature documentaries, though it's best to try to pick those that do not have human narration. If you do choose one with narration, you can incorporate the human narrator, actors, or subjects into the exercises as well.

Practice 9: Walk in Silence

Walking in silence is a practice that can nurture the five natural intelligences emphasized in this guide. The body reaps rewards, even if our cognitive processes harbor stress producing thoughts. Higher body esteem and health benefits are present even if you do not particularly want to go for a walk or think you would enjoy it. We can benefit by becoming aware of our thought processes that improve in silence. The human brain can track about 1.5 conversations at a time, and if we entertain inner chatter, we have less capability to process the relationships around us. We want to move our body while breaking older and often more restrictive thought patterns, such as self-judgment loops.

We've already explored thought and bodily sensation practices that help form new neurological pathways, or at least stretch the old ones. In the following exercise, the goal is to notice any thoughts that arise, and then let them go by breathing deeply. For just one breath (or more), discontinue what you were thinking about and instead use your senses to be in the world. In every bird walk I lead, I invite people to walk in silence for certain stretches of time, while aware of and loosely holding their thoughts. Often, I hear that this is the most enjoyable part of our time together.

Practice 10: Develop Your Own

Each of the previous practices are suggestions upon which you can build your own approach to growing your EI. Play and practice with this and let me know what you discover!

You can share what you have experienced privately by emailing One Earth Conservation at info@oneearthconservation.org, or by commenting on web pages at www.oneearthconservation.org, or on Facebook's page for One Earth Conservation or Birding for Life.

Notes

1. Garner H. *Frames of Mind: The Theory of Multiple Intelligences*. Basic Books: New York, NY. 2011.
2. Rosenberg M. *Nonviolent Communication: A Language of Life*. Puddle Dancer Press: Encinitas, CA. 2015.
3. Salovey P, Mayer JD. Emotional Intelligence. *Imagination, cognition and personality* 9(3): 1990. https://doi.org/10.2190/DUGG-P24E-52WK-6CDG
4. Goldman D. *Emotional Intelligence: Why It Can Matter More than IQ*. Bantam: New York, NY. 2012.
5. Turner JH. *The Origins of Human Emotions: A Sociological Inquiry in the Evolution of Human Affect*. Standford University Press: Redwood City, CA. 2000.
6. Barret LF. *How Emotions Are Made: The Secret Life of the Brain*. Mariner Books: Boston, MA. 2017.
7. Price A. Shut up and listen: Understanding the cold, hard truths behind the concept of empathy. Good. Last modified August 4, 2014. https://www.good.is/features/therapy-and-empathy
8. Zhang L, Yuan J. The effect of subconscious on life and ethical behavior. In: Bin MZ, Ghaffar NA, eds, *Proceedings of the 2021 4th International Conference on Humanities Education and Social Sciences*. ICHESS 2021. https://doi.org/10.2991/assehr.k.211220.172
9. Oliver M. *New and Selected Poems, Volume One*. Beacon Press: Boston, MA. 2004.
10. Burton J. *Conflict: Human Needs Theory*. Macmillan: New York, NY. 1990.
11. Danziger J, et al. Extraneous factors in judicial decisions. *Proc. Natl. Acad. Sci. U.S.A.* 108 (17): 2011. https://doi.org/10.1073/pnas.1018033108
12. White ME, et. al. The joy of birds: the effect of rating for joy or counting garden bird species on wellbeing, anxiety, and nature connection. *Urban Ecosyst* 26: 2023. https://doi.org/10.1007/s11252-023-01334-y
13. Burke J. The joy of birdwatching: research shows it can improve mental health and foster a sense of wellbeing. The Conversation. Last modified May 17, 2024. https://theconversation.com/the-joy-of-birdwatching-research-shows-it-can-improve-mental-health-and-foster-a-sense-of-wellbeing-229139

14. Sisgold S. *Whole Body Intelligence: Get Out of Your Head and Into Your Body to Achieve Greater Wisdom, Confidence, and Success.* Rodale Books: New York, NY. 2015.
15. Spector N. Smiling can trick your brain into happiness — and boost your health. NBC News. Last modified Nov 28, 2017. https://www.nbcnews.com/better/health/smiling-can-trick-your-brain-happiness-boost-your-health-ncna822591
16. Clayton S, Myers G. *Conservation Psychology: Understanding and Promoting Human Care for Nature.* Wiley-Blackwell: Hoboken, NJ. 2009.

Social Intelligence
Don't Flip Them the Bird

*You're an interesting species. An interesting mix.
You're capable of such beautiful dreams, and such horrible nightmares.
You feel so lost, so cut off, so alone, only you're not.
See, in all our searching,
the only thing we've found that makes the emptiness bearable,
is each other.*

– Carl Sagan[1]

What Is Social Intelligence?

We are always with others, and always connected to them. Our social brain is predisposed to wire itself around subconscious clues we derive from others so that we can resonate with them for our own benefit, theirs, the relationship's, and the greater group's. Even if we were to be in solitary confinement or alone on an island with no other living being, we are never alone because the "other" has been wired into our brain. It motivates our behavior and actions, whether we are conscious of it or not.

Our goal is to be more aware of how we are social beings and, therefore, to grow the possibility of choice both at the individual and group level, and foster deep connection with others. This awareness and the use of it is part of social intelligence. Social intelligence can also be defined as follows:

- The ability to get along well with others, and to influence them to cooperate with you for the benefit of the relationship and the greater group.
- The ability to be curious about the feelings and needs of others, and with this greater awareness of and connection to others, have a corresponding greater range of choices to produce healthy and productive relationships.

Social intelligence (SI) is an extension of EI because being aware of our own bodily states and emotions also tells us what others are feeling and needing. We have a much better chance to gain awareness of others and to hear their words if we still our own inner chatter. If we are having a complete inner dialogue with ourselves, especially an emotionally charged one, we have less room to listen to others. Growing our EI also grows our SI. Similarly, multispecies intelligence is related to SI and EI, for the more we know of ourselves and our species, the more we can know of other species. The reverse is also true. All three of these intelligences ask, "What are the feelings and needs present? What is the bodily state indicating?"

Each of us is born with social intelligence (SI), though some with more than others. After birth, our environment also influences our ability to socially interact with others at both the conscious and subconscious levels. As with emotional intelligence, no matter what characteristics we were born with or how we were nurtured, we each can move further along the continuum of greater social intelligence. Social intelligence is not just how we interact with others, but also our awareness of our own actions.

Benefits of Social Intelligence

Self-absorption in all its forms kills empathy, let alone compassion. When we focus on ourselves, our world contracts as our problems and preoccupations loom large. But when we focus on others, our world expands. Our own problems drift to the periphery of the mind and so seem smaller, and we increase our capacity for connection – or compassionate action.
- Daniel Goleman[3]

Individuals can grow their SI, and so can groups. There is good reason to grow SI, for individuals and groups that are the most socially intelligent are those that are capable of the following:

- Delivering greater care more quickly in more ambiguous situations
- Producing positive emotions that result in higher commitment to an organization
- Improving worker performance and satisfaction
- Having less stress, burnout, and compassion fatigue
- Having the greatest leadership ability[2]

Empathy is a hallmark awareness and skill in SI. If we can open ourselves to another's perspective, experiences, emotions, and needs, our relationships, communications, and organizations stand a greater chance of flourishing. Empathy doesn't require that we actually like the person we are with or even want to do something for them. Empathy just asks us to slow down enough to consider the other person's feelings and needs. Any opportunity to offer empathy in the present grows our ability to offer empathy in the future, even under trying circumstances (such as when our own needs are not being met).

Practicing empathy gives us a choice of when to offer empathy to one who might need it, even to ourselves when we are alone so that we can take in the beauty of others and the Earth. When opening ourselves up to the feelings and needs of others, we experience the interconnection that weaves our lives into all others. To live in empathy is to be held in a web of beauty.

Let's Make Up Shit Together

SI has a radical overtone that can change more than just our immediate relationships. As discussed in the EI chapter, our brains are virtuosos at making up stories about what we feel and need. Our brains interacting with others have constructed our own reality and the social reality of those around us. The stories we tell ourselves and others matter because they become our world. Studies have shown evidence of the Illusory Truth Effect, which is learning to believe in ideas that are repeated, even if when we first heard them we deemed them false.[4] For some, rationality cannot compete with repetition. If we repeatedly share amongst ourselves certain worldviews, stories, or feelings and needs, we will come to believe these as truth. We are who others tell us we are and how society categorizes us. Earth and Earth's beings are who we say or think they are. Repetition can define our world and pass this definition on to future generations. Neuroscientist Lisa Feldman Barrett said, "We construct a reality and give it to the future, so it behooves us to be as kind, compassionate, and as honest as we can so that we create the world we want to live in."[5]

David Brooks, a *New York Times* columnist, advises us similarly when he reflects on our species' propensity to create a world of our own making. He suggests that we humbly question everything we think and strive to compare our stories against the reality of others and science.[6] Miki Kashton, a leader in Non-Violent Communication, once said in a discussion I attended, "You can't believe anything you've been taught." If we construct our own social reality, why not base it on kindness, authenticity, and the needs of those in the biotic community in which we live?

Birding Is a Social Affair

We often observe or work with birds alongside other humans, or just happen to see them when we are out walking, traveling, or commuting. Even if we are alone, we really aren't because our brains have been formed around the experiences and stories of others. When we bird, we bird with the entire world. Just as we engage in inner chatter about ourselves, we "mind chatter" about others as well. Perhaps your inner chatter goes something like this:

- "Those politicians are jerks who have ruined our lives. This used to be an old growth forest and look at it now!"
- "That person isn't wearing a mask. What's wrong with them?"
- "Look at all that camera gear. Don't they know they are destroying the earth with their consumerism?"

Birds give us ample opportunity to be present and reframe how we think of others. It's not that others shouldn't be held accountable, but we want a world based on reality, not on stories that we or others have made up.

We also want to create the best opportunity to work with others in efficient and productive ways to heal our world, and especially with empathy. You don't have to believe, like, help, or spend time with a person, but you can honor the inherent worth and dignity of a biological creature trapped in a web spun by domination practices. We have more choices about how we interact with others and how we live and work together if we can recognize the bodily state of others and what that state says about their feelings and needs. Even if such insight is unknowable because of layers of neural wiring laid down by culture and experience, we can approach our understanding of others by improving our social intelligence.

Getting to Know You

I am often asked how we can know what another person or species is thinking if we aren't even sure about our own thoughts. Perhaps we can't know, but we can engage in a process that transforms the thoughts and behavioral patterns that are most harmful for ourselves and others. Humans have a propensity to judge those who are different, those not in our immediate social group, or those culturally identified in another group. This "othering" perhaps evolved to keep small social groups intact by uniting against a common enemy or competitor. Perhaps our social groups had to see other people as inherently bad to rationalize competing with them for resources. Harmful conflict probably began even before we became *Homo sapiens*, as evidenced with other primates who exhibit violent behaviors, most notably some of our closest relatives, the chimpanzees (*Pan troglodyte*).

At the same time, our bodies and minds are ready to establish patterns of collaboration and prosocial behavior, which are also evident in other primates. The image of our species as ruthless competitors in William Golding's novel *Lord of the Flies* is likely not based on fact. In the novel, boys are shipwrecked on an island, and violence and conflict quickly ensue. Contrary to this fictional narrative, a true event occurred when six boys from Tonga were shipwrecked in a borrowed boat on a deserted island in the Pacific for fifteen months. Rutger Breggman, author of *Humankind: A Hopeful History* wrote about this event, "The real Lord of the Flies is a story about friendship, operation, co-resilience, and hope."

But What About Our Enemies?

> *Observing without judging is the highest form of human intelligence.*
> – Attributed to J. Krishnamurti[7]

BIRDING FOR LIFE

There is no doubt that individuals and groups of people have caused great harm and suffering to other people and species, as well as to our planet. As so much of human behavior is subconscious and controlled by cultural whims and shared experiences, we might ask why we would work hard to understand others. This may seem even more confusing if we believe others are "out to get us" and there is no chance of finding common ground.

Because of our group mind and subconscious-influenced behaviors, we need to collaborate on this together to bring awareness of reality to our lives and reduce harm. We can ask questions about others to grow our SI, such as, "What are they feeling and needing? What more can I learn about our species and their culture in order to understand this situation?"

An example is my experience with people who poach parrots in the Americas. Working in parrot conservation for over 39 years, I have had my share of confrontations with and lamentations over poachers and the harm they cause to the endangered birds I work to protect. (To learn more about the development of my understanding of poachers, read *Conservation in Time of War*, a memoir of my early to middle years working in conservation.) I have chased them, argued with them, and criticized them. This negative thinking, as I suspected from early on, didn't serve me or our conservation efforts. True, sometimes protective actions and law enforcement are necessary, and people must be held accountable. However, my internal judging of them harmed me, and I suspected it adversely impacted the outcomes of our conservation projects.

I frequently recalled the life of Diane Fossey, who railed against poachers and was criticized for her treatment of and attitude about Africans. She was killed perhaps in part because of her defiant stance and lack of interpersonal skills. I had her in mind when I last approached an armed man hunting illegally in our parrot conservation areas. I thought then that there had to be a healthier way to build a better future where conservation is not a war between enemies.

One of our conservation leaders in Guatemala was killed in 2021 because he confronted parrot poachers near an active nest on his own ranch. The men arrested for the crime were heavily armed and were involved in a host of criminal activities. Likewise in Honduras, local community poachers threaten our parrot rangers frequently. It is perhaps true that many people who poach in many areas cannot be brought into right relationship, and no matter the SI intent of the project, solutions cannot be found to both address their needs and end the slaughter of birds, wildlife, forests, and people. Conservation needs a vision of peace. The underlying structures of domination and resource extraction we inherited from various cultures trigger unnecessary conflicts in the field. Ultimately the poacher is not the enemy, and neither are any of us trapped in an unjust and oppressive system.

To me, the easy and common approach is to make the poacher the identified enemy when, in fact, it is potentially within each of us to cause harm and be seduced and formed by our cultures. Upon closer analysis of these people who poach, especially the local community members, I found that they have similar needs to the conservationists.[8] Conservationists and poachers just choose different strategies to meet these needs, with some strategies being more harmful than others.

By empathizing with the people who poach, I find I have more choices about how to interact with community members. It also helps to consider a social analysis of the demand market for pets that fuels poaching and of colonialism and extraction economies. This deep dive into the lives of poachers helps me hold them less in contempt and more as worthy people with whom we struggle together to find a way towards a better future. Often these poachers become rangers and even friends, which they could never have done if I had continued to categorize them as the other. Our conservation outcomes and my own wellbeing improve as I learn to embrace and be embraced by reality.

Similarly, and in a less dramatic scenario than poaching, my relationships with family, friends, and colleagues have also improved, as has my resilience to stay engaged even when experiencing discomfort and risk. I feel a more vibrant connection to all of life by seeking to see humans for who we are – biological beings shaped by culture and experience. If I want future humans to be treated better and to treat themselves and other species better, I need to construct a social reality in every moment that invests faith in the inherent worth and dignity of every being. I do this by putting on my observer/biologist hat and asking what humans are thinking and feeling, and what I learn about them as an astute observer of human behavior. At the same time, I am also managing my inner dialogue so that I create space to be present to the reality around me.

Don't think, however, that I have arrived at any stage of enlightenment. The constant news of human conflict and harm, and of trees felled and parrots stolen, feels like getting kicked in the gut every day. I have anger, and I have judgment. But I also have a process that can keep me growing my connection to life and engagement while doing the hard work that must be done.

Flipping the Bird

So, what do people have to do with birds? Here's the thing. If we as conservationists are not invested in the innate beauty (and tragedy) of ourselves and others, we will follow the same old pathways by not investing in birds (and vice versa). We can expand our presence in reality by concentrating not just on any one species, but on as many as we can fit into our days, lives, and brains. Being outside birding and being in nature are gateways to increasing our connection and resilience. In that space, we can expand our results by including humans in hopes of seeing beauty, experiencing wonder and awe, and embracing reality.

When I first became a bird veterinarian, my approach to medicine was to consider not just the bird being treated, but the staff member who was treating them. Caring for birds and people together intensified when I started working in conservation in Guatemala, where the "bird problem" was immensely and directly tied to the "people problem." In caring for the birds, I had to care for the humans — and, indeed, I think I fell in love with humanity for the first time in the fierce arena of the civil war in Guatemala. Caring for one species is caring for the other, for the health of one is interconnected to the health of all.

People often ask why I work so much with people and not more with birds, as well as why I work with birds when there is so much human suffering. Indeed, I am sometimes torn between prioritizing either humans or birds in our conservation work. But this is a false dichotomy, a cultural presumption that there is a difference between caring for humans and other species. To truly love one, all must be loved, and to love all, each must be loved. And by love, I mean committing to humbly engage in learning about the other in order to improve life for all. We can tweak our brain's leanings away from believing old stories by focusing our attention on birds and humans. I can think of no better opportunity to do that than when sharing the marvel of both birds and humans during a birding event.

Birding and Social Intelligence Practices

Practice 1: Sharing This Perfect World: Growing SI Through Empathy

> (For this exercise, and for others, refer to the
> Feelings and Needs List in the Appendix)

This exercise might be one to do at the end of a bird walk, or during a walk at a time set aside for concentrating on humans. The amount of time for sharing per individual may range from one to fifteen minutes. I often suggest five minutes total to share this practice during long stretches where we would likely encounter fewer birds, such as the drive to a birding location or the walk back to the parking lot later in the day.

BIRDING FOR LIFE

1. Before beginning the dialogue, breathe deeply for a minute. Then, if possible, look to the ground, then to the sky, and then twirl around slowly with your arms outstretched. Smile as you come around to the original position, and then bow with both hands clasped together. (See the earlier explanation of why body movements are important to connection in the EI Practice, Practice 1: Birding Is Stretching Yourself.)
2. Choose one person to go first who will be the speaker. The others will be the listeners. The speaker will take the allotted time to describe their perfect world, the most beautiful world they can imagine. What would it feel, look, and smell like? What would people from various demographics be doing, feeling, and thinking? What would other species be doing, feeling, and thinking? What would the landscapes and ecological systems look like? What and how are people's relationships, families, work life, and hobbies like?
3. As each person talks, the others listen without interrupting or commenting. At the end, the listeners guess what the speaker felt while they spoke, and what needs are behind the speaker's description of their world. What needs are being met in this most beautiful world? What needs are most important to the speaker?
4. The speaker responds with whether the listeners' guesses resonate with them or not.
5. When ready, switch roles and a listener is now the speaker, repeating the guessing of feelings and needs at the end.
6. Once all have shared and received feedback, then each share how the exercise informed them, and what they are taking with them from it.
7. After completing this exercise, invite the others to breathe deeply for a minute.
8. If in a large group, pairs can describe their experience with this exercise to the group.

People's perceptions of this exercise vary widely, with some feeling uncomfortable with sharing and others forgetting to listen without interruption. Some may say that the world is entirely perfect just as it is and describe what they are perceiving in the moment. No matter how each person responds to the practice, the entire group and the facilitators listen to their experiences without offering advice or comments unless the speaker requests it.

Practice 2: Mourning This Perfect World

> *The ecologist (in a more than scientific sense) is someone who is touched by this loss in such a way as to mourn the toll of extinction instituted by human exemptionalism and exceptionalism. She is bereft and yet also understands that this feeling, her being touched by irrevocable loss, is itself a matter of realizing the existence of a sense of an ecological and ethical and political community with other species.*
>
> – Mick Smith[9]

Mourning is a radical act that helps us communally construct a social reality of the beauty and tragedy of our biotic communities. When we share the pain and loss we feel with others, our grief becomes a shared experience that not only lends comfort but also becomes a sharp lens through which we can better see reality. In doing so, we set the framework for a social undertaking to value life on this planet and do all we can to cherish it, protect it, and allow it to flourish in its own autonomous way.

Often, mourning together occurs spontaneously without a structured event or invitation. In this case, we are open to the possibility that our shared experience might take a different turn. Such moments to share grief are precious and lay the groundwork for a more connected, beautiful world. These moments might not occur while birding, but any time we experience loss and the opportunity to share it should not be missed.

BIRDING FOR LIFE

A missed opportunity to grieve occurred when I was nearly school age, still roaming the neighborhood as there was no kindergarten in our rural Tennessee community. One late afternoon, our pack of kids saw a flock of sparrow hawks, American kestrels, near our home. We raced after them and found an injured kestrel on the ground with a bloody, broken wing. We searched for my father to guide us to help the bird. He looked at the bird without saying a word, went into the house, and came out with his BB gun. When he raised the rifle to his shoulder, I pleaded with him to let the bird live and promised I'd take care of her. I screamed while he shot the bird again and again until she lay dead. He only said, "Go get a shovel." We buried the bird, and I cried for her and my father's disregard for life.

Years later, my father and I were offered the opportunity to rectify that earlier grief. My father asked me to run errands with him in town. Along a busy country road, we sighted a pair of yellow hammers, now called northern flickers. They are beautiful, large woodpeckers that totally captivated us as they flew in front of the car ahead of us, but one flicker didn't clear the road in time. The car kept going, and I expected my father to do the same, but he stopped. He walked to the dead flicker on the side of the road. Next to his body perched his mate. She refused to fly away even though we were nearby. I looked up to ask my father what we could do. He was crying, so I did too. Together, we grieved and healed in that moment.

During bird walks, I don't have a particular practice of mourning, but at the end of the walk I always close by inviting anyone to share something for which they were grateful or they mourned. Once, our group was gathered in a closing circle and sharing gratitude when one woman shared that it was the anniversary of her niece's death. Tears began to fall. Another woman spoke of how she lived with her son who wanted to kill himself because he was distraught at the callous acceptance of a dying planet by our society. Together, we can help hold the pain of such loss and construct meaning around how beautiful and wondrous a niece, a son, and our planet are. That shared sense of the preciousness of life strengthens us to be more resilient as we care for all beings, including ourselves.

A more structured format for mourning might proceed thus:

1. Invite those who are willing to take in the beauty of what is around them. Then, consider who or what we love that is not present or has been diminished from our lives. This could be a human friend or family member, an entire group such as native people or those enslaved or oppressed, extinct and endangered species, a companion animal, or a degraded or denuded ecosystem.
2. After several deep breaths, I invite the group to pair up and continue walking as they tell each other of their losses. Like in the sharing of the perfect world, the listener is fully and silently present until the speaker is finished. Then, without offering advice or summarizing the meaning, they may ask what the speaker wants, which might include the listener sharing their impression of the speaker's feelings and needs or summarizing what they heard. Once the speaker acknowledges that they feel heard, or if their body signals that they are ready to move on, then the pair switches roles and the other person shares their loss.
3. After this period, which can last five minutes or more, call the group back together and let people share their experiences of the exercise.

We spend time in mourning because it claims our hearts. In doing so, we help others claim their rightful place on Earth.

Practice 3: Ethno-ornithology

Not all these practices are the main activity during birding; they can also be used at home or at work. One of the practices that proved helpful for me as a conservationist was ethno-ornithology. This is the study of the relationship between people and birds. It combines anthropological, cognitive, and linguistic perspectives with natural sciences in order to describe and interpret how people perceive and use birds.[10] The basic premise is that the researcher undertaking the study is embedded into the group being studied, and as such their interactions become part of the process. Ethno-ornithology is one more way that EI practices merge with those of SI, as both develop curiosity about and acceptance of oneself and one's species.

Another underlying aspect of this field is that the degree to which a person or group values birds is not inherently "wrong," though their actions can cause great harm to birds. People value birds differently, but most assign a value to them. The goal of the researcher is to describe that group's values related to and their use of birds, while seeking to be an impartial observer of the harmful or helpful aspects of human behavior. The actions resulting from their values can have nurturing or harmful impacts on the birds, ecosystem, or people. But the researcher's underlying goal is to learn about the group, and that begins with a neutral description of the group's underlying values. We study groups not with the intent to judge them, but to understand them.

I first learned of this practice while auditing university classes, and I subsequently conducted an ethno-ornithological study on parrot conservationists in the Americas. Studying methodology includes embedding oneself into the culture, so I worked alongside parrot conservationists in many countries. Copious journal notes were logged, as were interviews and questionnaires. I compiled the most common words and values used about birds and the use of birds in conservation.

One of the strongest and most frequent values assigned to birds was that they provided income and a respectable job. Following close behind this was the value of teamwork, collecting data, and contributing to the community. Mentioned less often, but always present, were the values attributed to birds of beauty, freedom, interconnection, and love. Most of the bird conservationists I interviewed were local to the communities where conservation efforts were underway in Guatemala, Belize,

Honduras, and Nicaragua. Many of my contacts had been poachers with varied values ascribed to different species of birds. For example, some shot hawks that preyed on parrots and chickens, while simultaneously risking their lives to conserve parrots.

I learned in this study to step back from my reactions to people from different cultures with different values concerning birds. This has helped me stay engaged with people who treat birds quite differently than I do, even those who harm birds by poaching, trading, and caging them to keep as pets. I imagined myself as a dispassionate Werner Herzog filming a documentary about birds, always asking what was going on without steering the production into a projection of my biases, while still acknowledging my reactions to and judgements of what I experienced.

I recommend using the practice of ethno-ornithology to those who work in bird conservation, or any advocacy or social justice endeavors, to better understand both the researcher's own "group" and those considered "the other." Ethno-ornithology can help grow the researcher's curiosity and engagement with others to build productive alliances across the chasm of differences. At the same time, it can help the researcher understand that they are also part of the study, and can share their values and strategies with humility and honesty to maintain relationships between the groups and conservation coalitions.

There are resources for learning how to do ethno-ornithology,[11] which is a subset of ethno-biology,[12] and the results of some studies. What follows is an abbreviated practice.

1. Choose a group of people you would like to better understand and with whom you can share activities. This may be a local birding group or club, a hunter's association, or a conservation organization. It may also be the people with whom you share your enjoyment of birds, though you may wish to challenge yourself by selecting people whose views differ from yours.

2. Engage in at least one activity with this group, such as birding, farming, a meet-up at a zoo or conservation area, etc.
3. Observe their behaviors concerning birds and the environment, perhaps taking short notes while engaged and making longer journal entries at home. You could also keep you notetaking brief, though the more you invest, the more you learn. For instance, if out birding, note if people use smartphone apps or other resources to help identify the birds. Do they talk about the birds, or to them? What do they say and do during the activity? Include what your role was in these activities, as well as what you thought and felt.
4. Make a list of questions you'd like to ask each person. Perhaps it will just be one or two questions, such as, "Why did you come out birding today?" I present this question to the entire group before every walk so we can hear how people value birds and their habitats. You might also ask, "What do the birds mean to you? What bird-related activities do you engage in, such as hunting, feeding, conservation, eating, etc.?" One way to begin this exercise is to ask, what is your favorite bird and why? Or with which type of bird do you identify most and why? Listen openly without interruptions, except to ask for greater clarity.
5. When reviewing your notes, recordings, questionnaires, or journal entries, make a list of bird activities and a list of values attributed to the birds. Write a paragraph as if reporting your findings to an anthropology conference by addressing this question: What is the structure of these people's society in relation to valuing and interacting with birds? You are simply reporting, while also acknowledging your own actions, responses, and projections about these people. You are also objectively reporting on yourself.
6. Share this practice with others, for support and to deepen your findings and reflections. Answer these questions: What did this ethno-ornithological practice mean for me? How did I experience it? Is there anything I learned or want to do

differently? The goal of this exercise is to grow our curiosity and understanding of others so that we deepen our relationships with all of life, with particular attention to not demonizing or transferring enemy images upon those with whom we differ.

Practice 4: Being a Primatologist

This practice is much like the previous one in that you strive to be as much of an unbiased observer as you can. Of course, your experiences and stories are the filters through which you perceive the world and cannot be avoided. However, the intention here is to break through the stories that do not serve you or others. We want to share new stories and reduce harm. The goal is to learn about great apes – specifically, us humans — by imagining you are a primatologist trained to be suspicious of any hypothesis, methodology, or conclusions because you know humans tend to interpret the world with a biased view. This is why the scientific method requires repetition with different teams to weed out idiosyncratic human components.

Below is a shortened version of how to proceed with this practice, though you may wish to take this perspective every day. One method is to refer to humans as animals or great apes. This disrupts the stories of human exceptionalism that views people as either better or worse — or both — than other species, and moves beyond our knee-jerk socialization. Instead, we become socialized to see humans for who we are, beautiful yet tragic beings.

1. To begin, imagine you are a primatologist out in nature studying a troupe, family, or other gathering of primates. You might even imagine yourself as a primatologist you have heard of, such as Jane Goodall. You see yourself walking slowly, fully alert, with your journal or recorder in hand. Your eyes are wide open, and you are concentrating on your subjects: the people, who are also primates, gathering before you.

2. You watch and observe, making very little noise and interacting as little as possible with your subjects. Perhaps if you are out watching birds with other people, you might do this for a few minutes. You make notes (mental, written, or recorded) of their behaviors without assigning meaning to what might be motivating them.
3. Your thoughts and notes are objective, such as, "Juvenile human jumps twice upon seeing an osprey fly over with two fish in its talons. Their mother smiles as her eyes follow the bird over the lake. She places her hand on her child's shoulder. Child turns to her and laughs." Later, you might interpret this scene by speaking of the humans' wonder and awe, and their sharing of this with others using touch and laughter. You can make a list of what they might be feeling and needing.
4. Continuing with this example, to augment your study, you research this species by reading or listening to books, articles, and documentaries on awe and wonder in primates, the impact of nature and birds on people and social bonds, and the physiology of unconscious body movements such as jumping, smiling, and laughing. Extend your study to other great apes, including extinct human species. What is evolution's role in this range of behaviors?
5. You could deepen your study by repeating the study to observe what other groups of people do when they see birds. You could gather more information regarding the same two individuals by asking them about their experience when the osprey flew over.

I have found this shorthand of human behavior helpful when I work with people who are different from me and whom I judge — which is just about every human, considering the harm our species has done, is doing, and will do. These exercises bring some ease, relief, and even humor to what might be untenable situations in which I find myself enmeshed with others as we pursue solutions to our individual and collective needs. My spouse and I have over the years, used a shortened form of this practice by touching one another and hooting like chimpanzees when we found ourselves caught up in our dramas. It reminds us that we are humans, one great ape species among many, all vulnerable and precious. Though we might not be in control of much, we can love who we and others are, at least for the next moment. Over time, such reframing leads to permanent changes in our thoughts and behaviors.

Practice 5: Laugh and the Whole World Laughs With You

In the EI section, we considered how laughter is good for individuals. It also is good for groups of people. It can increase creativity, productivity, communication, empathy, and cooperation. Laughter also creates and deepens social bonds. We share laughter with other species of great apes, and its presence in some form originated 10 to 16 million years ago. We laugh as a socially complex primate, and we can co-opt this behavior to serve us well.

Because of its positive effects, laughter is intentionally used to bond and motivate groups, and to deepen individual and group social and emotional intelligences. One such practice is to ask everyone to "fake laugh" for a period of time. Admittedly, this can be awkward, especially with groups of relative strangers, but other practices exist, especially revolving around birds. Here are some ideas:

1. In any situation, seek to find the humor in it, perhaps punning or quipping about a shared experience. Some people are more naturally able to tap into humor than others, but the ability to make others laugh can be learned.
2. Before going out in nature with a group of people, make a list of bird puns to share. Invite others to come up with their own puns. Sources of puns abound on the internet.[13,14]
3. Consider sharing a humorous anecdote about a bird or nature experience while enjoying birds or nature with someone else. Also, think of a weird attribute of birds that

might lead people to experience wonder, and perhaps comic relief. Here are two favorites that I used on a bird walk:

A flock of geese flew over in a lopsided V, and I asked the group why they thought one side of it was longer than the other. People suggested wind resistance, avoiding predators, etc. I told them my grandfather, a man of the winter wilds in Wisconsin, taught me the following insight years ago: "One side of the V is longer because there are more birds in it." The image of my grandfather teasing me with this as a child increases their amusement.

Another tidbit I share is the size of male birds' testicles increasing during the spring in North America. This nugget seems appropriate when we talk about migration, the increase of bird song in the spring, or territoriality around nesting season. I tell them male birds have internal testes so we cannot see them, but a lot is going on in there. During the winter's short days, bird testicles decrease in size, and with spring's longer days, the testes size increases. I ask them to guess how much larger they grow. After a few guesses, I share that robins' testicles can enlarge up to 500 times. I don't usually need to say anything else as guffaws and bawdy jokes increase exponentially.

4. After a bird walk, I ask the group to stand in a circle, and I offer them plush birds. They can toss the birds to one another and call out the species of birds they saw, or the needs and feelings they experienced. Tossing birds often goes awry, and people get softly bonked in the process. With children this is particularly fun and often results in aimed tossing.

Practice 6: Closing Gratitude and Checklist

Practicing gratitude is good for us as individuals and groups. Gratitude has contagious and enduring consequences. It can improve sleep quality and emotional regulation; increase feelings of happiness and positivity; foster hope; reduce stress, burnout, and trauma; deepen relationships; enhance physiological and physical health; develop our empathy and resilience; and decrease aggression.[15,16]

I invite people to share gratitude at the end of most events I facilitate. This can also be done while sharing birds or nature with others. People often remember the last things shared in a group and carry that emotional impact with them. It is important to share gratitude, preferably at the end of the event.

Part of a gratitude practice is to list all the species we saw, and share which were especially remarkable for each person. By naming the species, we honor them, give thanks, and perhaps report our sightings on eBird[17] or iNnaturalist.[18]

We also deepen our gratitude for birds by growing our Multispecies Intelligence and bringing that into the next session.

Notes

1. Sagan C. Contact. Pocket Books: New York, NY. 1997.
2. Goleman D, Boyatzis, RF. Social intelligence and the biology of leadership. *Harvard Business Review* 86(9). 2008.
3. Goleman D. Social Intelligence: The New Science of Human Relationships. Bantam Books: New York, NY. 2006.
4. Udry J, Barber SJ. The illusory truth effect: A review of how repetition increases belief in misinformation. *Current Opinion in Psychology* 56. 2024. https://doi.org/10.1016/j.copsyc.2023.101736
5. Barret LF. *How Emotions Are Made: The Secret Life of the Brain.* Mariner Books: Boston, MA. 2017.
6. Brooks D. Is self-awareness a mirage? *New York Times* September 16, 2021. https://www.nytimes.com/2021/09/16/opinion/psychology-consciousness-behavior.html
7. Antiglio D. How to observe your thoughts without judgment. Accessed November 18, 2024. https://be-sophro.com/blog/learning-to-observe-your-thoughts-without-judgement/
8. Joyner L. Needs of poachers and conservationists. One Earth Conservation. Last modified May 30, 2017. https://www.oneearthconservation.org/post/2017/05/30/needs-of-poachers-and-conservationists
9. Smith M. Ecological community, the sense of the world, and senseless extinction. *Environmental Humanities* 2 (1), 2013. https://doi.org/10.1215/22011919-3610333
10. Ethno-ornithology. Wikipedia. Last modified December 28, 2023. https://en.wikipedia.org/wiki/Ethnoornithology
11. Tidemann S, Gosler A (eds). *Ethno-ornithology: Birds, indigenous peoples, cultures and society.* Earthscan: Oxford, Oxfordshire, United Kingdom. 2019.
12. Nabhan GP (ed). *Ethnobiology for the future: Linking cultural and ecological diversity.* Arizona University Press: Tucson, AZ. 2016.
13. The Very Best 82 Bird Puns. Ponly. Accessed November 15, 2024. https://ponly.com/bird-puns/
14. 231 Funny Bird Puns and Jokes for Kids. Celebrate and Have Fun. Accessed November 15, 2024. https://katyskidcorner.com/bird-puns/

15. Smith JA, et al (eds). The gratitude project: How the science of thankfulness can rewire our brains for resilience, optimism, and the greater good. New Harbinger Publications: Oakland, CA. 2020.
16. Ackerman CE. Benefits of Gratitude: 28+ Surprising Research Findings. Positive Psychology. Last modified April 12, 2017. https://positivepsychology.com/benefits-gratitude-research-questions/
17. eBird. Cornell Lab of Ornithology. Accessed November 15, 2024. https://ebird.org/home
18. iNaturalist. Accessed November 15, 2024. https://www.inaturalist.org/

Multispecies Intelligence
Be the Bird

What happens to them matters to them.
— Tom Regan[1]

Introduction

    Multispecies Intelligence (MI) is a form of Social Intelligence (SI) beyond the human species. MI is the ability to be curious and knowledgeable about the motivations, subjective experience, behavior, and welfare status of other species to maximize benefit and minimize harm for them. In the previous intelligences, Emotional Intelligence (EI) and SI, we don't include their purposes in their definitions. The lists of the positive impacts of EI and SI imply that we develop them to help ourselves and other people. However, we humans often lag behind in our conception of other species being worthy of moral concern, or a mutualistic or interconnected relationship. The definition of MI spells this out so that we can understand why this intelligence is of importance — not just to humans, but to the rest of life around us.

Born a Bird

We are always in relationship to something. It is in discovering a wise and compassionate relationship to all things that we find a capacity to honor them all.
— Jack Kornfield[2]

Every human is born with MI, just as we are with SI that speaks to human interactions. We innately focus on others, be they humans or other species, as our young brains discover who we are by being in relationships. Who we think of as the self is actually a bunch of neural wirings created by relationships. Infants have been studied thoroughly in this regard, and their emotional and mental development depends on who they relate to in their environment, usually quite strongly with parents but also with animals and trees. Their sense of self, called the ecological self, depends on who is in their environment, interactions, and relationships. The self is the brain weaving itself into a web of relationships. This worked on a meta level as human species' physiology evolved around the environment, exerting selection pressure on our genes. This means that we are hard-wired, as well as culturally and developmentally prone, to be part of both the human group and the wider ecological community.

Antone Martinho-Truswell, a behavioral ecologist and author of the book *The Parrot in the Mirror: How Evolving to Be Like Parrots Makes Us Human*, theorizes that the challenges of life on Earth — indeed, the ache of physical suffering and death — caused birds, especially parrots, and humans to develop similar traits in a process called "convergent evolution." We both are social and smart, live long lives, move around mostly in the day, and raise our young more like birds than many other mammals.

In *Avian Illuminations*, author Boria Sax similarly addresses how humans are like birds, but his conclusions are rooted in nonbiological causes. His theory is that humans' close relationships to birds shaped our culture and human identity. With one example after another, he shows how intimately our bonds with birds are bound up in the matrix of ideas, practices, fears, and hopes that form human civilization. People from the earliest times followed birds for orientation, especially on large bodies of water, as well as to find destinations that would host a new home. Stories and myths built around this practice include the founding of Yamato by following a mystical crow, of Mexico City by following an eagle, and very possibly of London by following ravens. He concludes that a world without birds would effectively mean the end of humankind, for they not only tell us how we got to be who we are, but also who we might yet become.

Listening and paying attention to everyone in our environment tells us who we and others are. We are not our own; others formed us. Birds formed us. Earth formed us. Multispecies intelligence isn't about becoming the bird, but about gaining awareness that we are already the bird.

You Say PILL-eated, I Say PIE-leated

What is the correct way to say pileated woodpecker? No matter how we pronounce it, we know that the words point to a large North American woodpecker. Or do we? When we see a large black and white woodpecker, we may call it an ivory-billed woodpecker, while others may call it a pileated. Which bird is it? Others know the ivory-billed woodpecker as the Lord God bird. They are then assured that this species is not yet extinct, that they have seen it, while others say the evidence is flimsy and the bird is extinct. Which is it?

Several authors have mused about how some people report seeing the bird, while others who are present do not. Our brains are not only capable of filling in the missing pieces of a visual observation, but also of making up stories to explain what just happened. This means that when we engage with the natural world, we are prone to all kinds of errors, so we need a way to check our assumptions and guesses against what a bird truly is.

This is where MI helps us not only expand our narrow personal and species outlook, but also shift our relationships with others.

David Brooks, a *New York Times* columnist, researched how humans make up stories about why they feel what they do, and why they do what they do.[3] He mused:

> "One of the most unsettling findings of modern psychology is that we often don't know why we do what we do. ... People will concoct some plausible story, but often they really have no idea why they chose what they did. ... Maybe we can't know ourselves through the process we call introspection. But we can gain pretty good self-awareness by extrospection, by closely observing the behavior of others. We can attain true wisdom and pretty good self-awareness by looking behavior and reality in the face to create more accurate narratives. In telling ever more accurate stories about ourselves, we send different beliefs, values, and expectations down into the complex nether reaches of our minds, and — in ways we may never understand — that leads to better desires, better decision-making and more gracious living."

David Brooks refers to human species, but his point also relates to other species — including, of course, birds. Multispecies intelligence can aid us in having more reality-based narratives of other species in our world. The goal is to grow our shared reality and experiences of birds, no matter the words, ideology, or politicized subjects that cleave us from our interconnections to one another.

Two Errors With Multispecies Intelligence

To grow our MI, we need to be aware of the limitations of our conscious, culturally derived mind that separates humans from other species and each other. We evolved to see those of a competing group as "distinct and different others." This in turn grows the strength of our own group's relationships, so that our family or small group is stronger and can protect more resources for ourselves. One check to this "othering" and inherent tribalism is to develop our MI, which uses EI, communication, and behavior across species' lines for the mutual benefit of all. It requires understanding species' needs, behaviors, motivations, and interconnecting relations with others and their habitats. In short, we ask: what is the individual feeling and needing?

We do this in part by seeking to know the motivations for behaviors, such as understanding their subjective experience (emotions and internal processing) and needs. This means employing what is known as critical anthropomorphism, the study of animal behavior by using the sentience of the observer to generate theories based on the knowledge of the species, its perceptual world, and ecological and evolutionary history.

By engaging in critical anthropomorphism, we avoid two errors on either end of the spectrum of multispecies understanding. One error is to say that other species are nothing like humans (anthropocentrism), and the other is to say they are exactly like us (uncritical anthropomorphism). Critical anthropomorphism means that we imagine what it is like to be in the shoes, paws, hooves, claws, or feet of another, and then check if we might have made either of the two errors. We first put on our scientific lens and ask what this individual is feeling and needing. We then put on our empathetic, embodied lens and repeat the same question. We employ all the available science, and sensory and body resonance to study, reflect, and discuss. We then check our assumptions. Finally, we ask how our perceptions of another might lead to more harm than good.

No Better

The one historical constant in my field is that each time a claim of human uniqueness bites the dust, other claims quickly take its place.
— Frans de Waal[4]

A prime example of how we wrongfully see humans in multispecies communities is the statement, "Humans are the only ones who…(use tools, grieve, have culture, etc.). Throughout my lifetime I have seen culturally dominant and even scientific views that state this viewpoint be refuted. A classic example is when in college, I was taught that only humans use tools. Now we know that a variety of animals use tools, and not just primates that use rocks to access food. Birds of all kinds use tools, including crows who fashion sticks to gain access to food and parrots who pick up sticks to bang out forest-penetrating sounds on trees.

Be cautious or suspicious if ever you hear or are tempted to say:

- "Only humans do X."
- "Humans have greater choice or similar behaviors for different reasons."
- "What sets humans apart from animals …"

Ask yourself if such wording is to promote human exceptionalism, the idea that humans are better than other animals.

For instance, humans aren't the only ones with prosocial behaviors. In other animals we have documented traits such as empathy, caring for others, coparenting, grieving, befriending, and playing.

No Worse

This dualism is an act of severing, a foundational, traumatic fissure between, to put it in stark Lacanian terms, reality (the human-correlated world) and the real (ecological symbiosis of human and nonhuman parts of the biosphere).
- Timothy Morton[5]

There is another kind of human exceptionalism in which humans aren't considered to be better than others because of their behaviors and intent, but rather worse. How many times have you heard, "Humans are so bad, we are the only ones who..." (cause climate change, commit murder, commit sexual violence, etc.). We need to be suspicious of this too because such generalizations reflect a homogeneous understanding of humans, as if the definition of the human species defines all individuals. How we define "human" is interlaced with ideologies and politics that serve an agenda, which may or may not be conscious. Our goal is to describe what is happening as objectively as possible, without making broad sweeping generalizations.

Let's take climate change, for example. There is no doubt that humans are causing great harm to Earth through our practices that emit pollutants and gases into the air, changing the climate and causing rising seas. Other species have also done so. About three billion years ago, Earth's atmosphere contained no oxygen, and anaerobic bacteria (those that can thrive without oxygen) were a predominant life form. Other species of bacteria evolved, such as cyanobacteria (blue-green algae) that produced oxygen as waste. This changed Earth's atmosphere and climate, causing a cooling Earth and a great die-off of anaerobic and aerobic bacteria alike.[6] This extinction paved the way for the successful evolution of many other species, including multicellular species and, later, complex animals and plants. One group of these species is trees, which interact with the environment and, in a recent study, reportedly caused or contributed to another great extinction in the Devonian

Period (419 to 358 million years ago).[7] In the late Devonian Period, 70% of species went extinct.

More examples of how other species are known to harm include sexual coercion, murder, cannibalism, infanticide, and war. The first four have been documented in birds.

Only Means Lonely

Whether we see humans as far better or worse than other species, or when we say that about any other species, we are committing multispecies errors. These include distancing from ourselves and others, fostering harm to others, and inviting despair, depression, and debilitating disconnection that disempowers us. We must ask why it is important to state that humans are fundamentally different from all other species. What is the intent? Is it a politicized technique to support or motivate certain human behavior? Why do we need to elevate or diminish one species over or below the other? Perhaps it helps us make sense of the world. Indeed, we have a biological propensity to compare and categorize as we have evolved to do this quickly to stay alive and maintain cohesive, small communities. Is the "other" someone I can trust? Will they care for me? Must I care for them? How harsh can I treat them? Can I take their resources, harm them, or eat them?

But most of us don't operate in isolated small communities anymore and instead interact with a global community of different species. We risk seeing other species as fundamentally different at our own peril because multispecies communities have evolved with a variety of actors, each of which provides niche contributions. By diminishing the wellbeing of even one keystone species, many others could fall into oblivion.

For instance, we know that under the ecological principle of trophic cascade, some species' actions help (or hurt) many others. The first of two key examples are wolves in North America that hunt grazers such as elk. Wolves, through hunting, lower grazers' numbers so that creek banks can flourish with native vegetation and healthy hydrology that help a variety of other species. The second example is sea otters that keep urchins in check by consuming them, which in turn allows kelp forests to thrive as well as the species that depend on them.

In both cases, we might think that wolves are the only ones that can keep down elk numbers, or otters are the only ones that keep down sea urchin numbers. However, we don't know if either is true. Other animals could move into those niches and impact the concentrations of prey. And why do we use the word "only?" In this case, it might be because we want to protect wolves and otters. It might be because we and many others need and depend on them, even the urchins and elk for population control. Though predation is hard on the hunted, an ecosystem that becomes unbalanced with too many of any one species could lead to a crisis that would harm other species, as is the case with humans today. But "only" in the English language invites the isolation of a particular occurrence or species. To correct this rampant "othering," discontinuing the use of "only" reduces categorizing one species compared to humans or each other. We can then describe what we are seeing without judging a species' attributes.

With a nonjudgmental lens, we can see how using "only" might celebrate the uniqueness of an individual, a species, or a community. This may be why authors often write that humans are the only ones who build great cathedrals of stone, a true marvel of human ingenuity. But we could also say that "only" leaf cutter ants farm fungus underneath their large earthen mounds. The use of "only" as proof of superiority invites separation and disconnection, while the goal of MI is to bridge the divisiveness we have learned. Deleting "only" from our practice creates the opportunity to witness the impact on our thinking and actions.

MI asks us all to be naturalists, if not scientists, who acutely observe the world around us and delay any conclusions that arise from our own biased thinking rather than from reality. Besides "only," "always" and "never" also discourage our openness to discovery.

Not Knowing

To grow our MI, we want to describe what we saw, studied, or observed, or what reality has proven to be fact. At the same time, we learn not to rely on our narrative selves who cannot sense every detail, and who make up stories about what has occurred. But if MI is knowing about other animals, what do we do if we cannot understand them enough to recognize what they are feeling and needing in order to reduce anthropogenic harm? Our working definition of MI is to ask what others are feeling and needing through observations and study, and to make guesses on motivations that lead to the fulfillment of needs. Can we know the interior subjective experiences and motivations of another person, or even ourselves, let alone an individual of another species? We may offer hope by being open to the vulnerability of not knowing

This very not knowing is what connects us to life. Boundaries dissolve between us and other species or individuals, between who we are as beings and all others who live within our DNA and make up the ecosystems on which we depend. Tim Morton, philosopher and author of *Humankind,* offers that our inability to know much of anything concretely reminds us that we are not superbeings, and that the tragedy of death and messiness of life are what connect us.[5] This connection is a deep empathy, and as we grow our awareness that we are not alone or isolated, we exceed our previous limitations in MI. Our MI comes from our bodies that are experientially immersed in a not-knowing state.

For example, other species have different senses and different acuities of their perceptions than humans do. Furthermore, we do not know how their brains are wired and cannot fathom their subjective experience. Ed Yong, in *An Immense World,* offers example after example of how animals sense through touch, taste, smell, hearing, vision, and magnetoreception.[9] Birds have cells that can pick up minute changes in Earth's magnetic field, which guides them in migration and seasonal movements. Each animal also has a specific proprioceptive system, which enables them to respond to stimuli that tell them their position, posture, equilibrium, and internal condition. Animals can inhabit and move about in water, trees, and air in ways we cannot. They sense the world and their place in it at levels we humans can only imagine through observation and study. But our not knowing invites us to envision a grander, more welcoming world.

To grow our MI, we may also follow author Lisa Barret's example by simplifying how we describe basic human emotion.[8] A body has a subjective experience that is made up of an arousal level (low to high) and a bodily response to move towards pleasantness or away from unpleasantness. Our body's interoception system lets us know how pleasant or calm an experience is and inputs these signals into every decision we make. Using words, such as mad and sad, to describe our experience is a human construct based on language. When using words to describe feelings or emotions in other animals, we are just sharing information between a specific subset of humans who have their own cultural contexts to explain subjective states. Barret suggests that to counteract our descriptive words that could be erroneous, we must try to understand animals' minds and behaviors based on their species and individual specific niche in the world, and explore what is occurring in others, no matter the species. By doing so, we construct reality based as much as possible on the other's experience instead of a human's limited view.

We enhance our MI by focusing on the answers to what others are needing and feeling with the basic questions: What is their arousal level, and do their bodies want to move away from or towards pleasantness? Pleasantness is not often used to help us conceive what our needs might be, so I will also ask this question in another way: How is an individual moving away from harm and towards benefit?

As humans, we assign words to describe the feelings and needs of "others," knowing that what we are communicating is a human construct about other species. By realizing this and gaining more knowledge and experience through not knowing, we develop a language that hones our observational and reporting skills to a level that is as nonjudgemental as possible. We can also develop a common language and shared reality based more on the "others" to explore the wellbeing of all — including animals, ourselves, and each other. Accepting our own animality, we can say that humans are truly exceptional, as are the bonobo, mantis shrimp, and peregrine falcon. Exceptional, yes. Superior, no.

Precautionary Guesses

When I was a senior in veterinary school in the mid-1980s, I was in the ICU as part of a rotation of orthopedic surgery. A dog was recovering from anesthesia after a complex hip surgery and was howling nonstop in her cage. I asked the resident if the dog was in pain and he said, "That is just the dog reacting to anesthesia. They don't feel pain like we do." I was very suspicious of his answer, and for good reason. During those years there were very few studies on the use of pain medication in animals, and I was not taught how to systemically treat pain in any animal. Now a plethora of studies on pain reception and management in a variety of species is available, and veterinarians routinely consider the animals' experiences of pain or suffering in any treatment regimen.

Humans made a big mistake in guessing about pain in animals. It is true that we cannot know exactly what they feel, even if after years of study we know the density and kind of receptors they have that sense noxious stimuli. We can guess at their nociception (ability to sense these adverse stimuli) in many species, but it is an even further reach to know how their minds process these inputs that result in sensing pain. Studies have shown that certain species seem to have a high tolerance for pain, though we can't absolutely know if they are experiencing discomfort or suffering.[9] For instance, naked mole-rats can tolerate high levels of carbon dioxide and low levels of oxygen, both of which send most species scurrying for a more livable environment than the dark tunnels of the mole-rats. The grasshopper mouse hunts scorpions and seems to shrug off stings from its prey as its nociceptors quit firing when scorpion venom is detected.

Even with these limitations in our depth of knowledge, if we put ourselves into the body of that moaning dog limping and yelping when she tries to walk, a good guess is the dog — a vertebrate relatively closely related to humans — is feeling pain. Using precaution as our guide, and knowing human hubris and the long history of regrettable mistakes in the past, we can make a more informed guess as to whether animals are being harmed or are harming.

In the 1980s, most veterinarians were using anesthesia when performing surgery. But there were periods of time when not only animals, but also human babies were cut open without anesthesia. The belief was that babies' expression of pain was reflexive, and the immaturity of the infant brain made the pain inconsequential. Perhaps, too, doctors didn't want to risk chemical anesthetic agents that would import risk to the child.

We now know that a variety of species, even invertebrates[10] and insects,[11] show behaviors indicative of anxiety and pain, and that their behaviors can be modified by administering human antianxiety medications and analgesics. This suggests that a variety of species have similar pathways in their bodies as do humans for anxiety and pain, and that they can experience low welfare. These studies and others, along with common sense, suggest that if we must make a guess about the wellbeing of another, we must be precautionary so that we err on the side of offering as much benefit and as little harm as possible.

Guessing Wrong on Intelligence

When I was a child, the phrase "bird brain" inferred that not only were birds dimwitted, but so was the targeted human. Since then, we have learned so much about avian intelligence and neurology that to be called a bird brain is now understood to be a high compliment. It turns out that though avian brains are smaller than many mammals', they don't need a brain as big because they have smaller bodies. Also, size is not the distinguishing measure of cognitive intelligence; how the brain tissue is organized is. What we didn't understand when I was a child is that the neural tissue in many bird species is densely packed, so they have more intelligence per gram of tissue. We also thought that since their brains don't have folds in their cortex, they were not highly intelligent. Turns out that through the process of convergent evolution, birds organized and evolved their pallium (forebrain) in ways that were different from mammals, but still highly effective in intelligence capacity.

Making Smarter Guesses About Intelligence

We need some clarification before our conception of avian intelligence is free to soar. The foremost point is that the level of intelligence of any individual in any species is not an indication of inherent worth and dignity. Perhaps being smart is something we admire and relate to as humans. Intelligence moves us to marvel at others, but we can also be easily amazed at the many other attributes that a species expresses, or simply its very existence on the planet. Even if we have a tough time perceiving complex behavior that we have in common as something we can admire in others, this should not diminish our respect for their wellbeing. Tom Regan says an individual of any species is like a cup. It is already a beautiful individual even though we humans have a propensity to try and fill the cup with descriptors that define the individual.[1] We might want to describe them by comparing them to human intelligence or prosocial or antisocial behaviors. However, the cup already exists in beauty without the human gaze. Perhaps we can celebrate this as we would a toast, raising the worth of another ever higher in a communal celebration of beauty and dignity.

Another aspect of researching intelligence is exploring the many different kinds of intelligences, even within one species. As discussed previously, in humans there are several intelligences, such as the five we are highlighting in this book: emotional, social, multispecies, ecological, and spiritual. There is also body-kinesthetic, verbal-linguistic (the ability to communicate), spatial (the ability to observe the world with the mind's eye), and logical-mathematical (the ability to solve mathematical problems). Birds and other animals also express these kinds of intelligences, but perhaps not at the same level or in the same way that humans do. A bat might be adept at forming an image from sounds it emits in the process of echolocation. A human brain would be challenged to do so, although some people with reduced vision do use clicks and sounds to map out their locations. A squirrel or a scrub jay can remember where they buried thousands of nuts or seeds, while the average North American spends 2.5 days a year looking for lost items.[12]

Studying intelligence is not without its pitfalls. Some scientists who study animals remark that species or individuals aren't easily motivated to participate in experiments. Scientist Ed Yong, when interviewed for his book *An Immense World*, referred to his studied animals — mantis shrimps — as spiteful because they didn't engage consistently in experiments.[9] They didn't eat very often and got bored, so he could work with them only once a day. There is also the problem of small sample sizes. For instance, it is hard to do statistical analysis on 100 elephants in a laboratory, especially with the inevitable variability between individuals.

Tests for animal intelligence often fail to replicate the animal's natural ecological context and are difficult to quantitate. For example, the mirror test doesn't easily cross species lines. In this test, a mark such as a piece of white tape is placed upon an animal, who is then given a mirror. If the animal focuses on the mark by pecking at it or rubbing it, the animal is said to have self-awareness. However, this may not work with animals who are not visually centered. For example, dogs interpret the world remarkably well through smell but "fail" the mirror test. If different tests were used for bodily awareness and the ability to identify oneself through scent, dogs would pass the self-awareness test.

By changing how we define animal intelligence and remembering how much we just don't know for certain, we can make more educated guesses about a species' characteristics.

Animal intelligence is the combination of skills and abilities that allows animals to adapt to and live in their native environments. We may ask what the animal is doing, thinking, sensing, and feeling, and if what they are doing is good for their own welfare or that of their species.

In summary, it seems that comparing any animal intelligence or other attribute against other species doesn't make sense. If we do, we invite a world of assumptions and projections. Earth is not a mirror that reflects only us. Many bird species are highly intelligent and are more than just feathered flying apes. They are beings unto themselves.

Addressing Human Domination With the Five Domains

If we are growing our MI in order to assure the best possible welfare of other species, we are challenged to measure their welfare status. Measuring seems impossible without using the lens of human perception. Everything we think and do filters through human perception, either our thoughts or our bodily states. However, we have tools to hone our MI skills. These include slowing down to observe and experience, as well as centering our observations to study, reflect, and test our hypothesis about the state of another.

We can use welfare science as an example. The Five Domains Model, a system used to assess an animal's welfare as objectively as possible, is made up of five categories: nutrition, environment, health, behavior, and mental state.[13] The latest version of the model adds a layer of human-nonhuman interactions to help us learn the impact of our relationships with others.

Recently, I was part of a research grant team that looked at the population status of parrots in Suriname, one of the two countries in the Americas where it is still legal to trap wild parrots and sell them internationally. The granting authorities asked us to produce a document listing trapping guidelines. I already knew there was no way to trap a wild bird and cage it without severely impacting its welfare, but what I hadn't done is document that science and information for others. So I reviewed the literature, and applied the Five Domains Model to the parrot trade for others to see what they could do to improve the lives of parrots while trapped, transported, and held in quarantine.[14] The conclusion of this position paper asserted that there is no way to ensure adequate welfare for parrots in captivity, knowing that Suriname and the world would continue to trade parrots and keep them in captivity.

Birds are not all cared for equally in captivity. Some people go to amazing lengths to ensure that their bird has the greatest choices and relative freedom to live in conditions that satisfy what they consider to be the bird's physiological and mental needs. However, whatever the situation of the bird, there is always room for improvement. The hope is that the tools in the Five Domains Model can help people not only make improvements but also guide them to care for parrots in situations that cannot be adequately or quickly improved, and to help move the behemoth of human domination further up the compassion and caring trail.

For instance, in the behavior category of the Five Domains, I outlined the circumstances we needed to analyze to determine the welfare status of a population of birds in captivity. I used an example of parrots held captive in the wildlife trade.

1. Invariant, barren environments (ambient, physical, or biotic) where parrots have markedly restricted choices and constraints on environmental-focused activity may be harmful. These include being housed in the same cage at all times, being in a restricted outdoor location or holding area, being unable to move variable distances in a day or to fly, or having no engaging choices (such as exploration or foraging). Low ranking in these categories can result in lack of agency, boredom, depression, withdrawal, neophobia (the fear of anything new), and stereotypic behaviors. Positive conditions, on the other hand, lead to necessary mental and physical stimulation, such as being pleasantly occupied and in good health due to a varied environment

where behavioral choices are enhanced, enjoyment of novelty exists, and a sense of being in control is dependable.
2. Inescapable sensory impositions — such as vocalizations of humans and other species nearby or increased amplitude from many voices during transport and holding — may lead to stress and lack of agency. Positive conditions lead to congenial sensory inputs and calmness.
3. Constraints on animal-to-animal interactive activity — such as being housed apart from conspecifics (members of the same species) or chosen flock members, friends, or mates — may lead to boredom, depression, stagnation, lack of sexual and reproductive activity, lack of bonding, frustration, general lack of good health, and reduced physical activity. Positive conditions lead to necessary stimulation, good health, parental rewards, excitation, playfulness, sexual gratification, and affectionate sociability.
4. Limits on threat avoidance, escape, or defensive activity — such as when caught in a trap or housed outside in a cage vulnerable to predators — will increase anxiety, sap energy, and can result in hypervigilance, anger, and possible physical harm. Positive conditions lead to a sense of safety, calmness, confidence, comfort, enjoyment of novelty, and good health.
5. Limitations on sleep and rest — such as in enclosures where birds cannot escape other species making noise or invasive movements, or in areas with no quiet time during the day or full darkness at night — may lead to physical and mental illness. Positive conditions lead to refreshment and energy.

I have couched this assessment in clinical terms and perhaps have impacted your own welfare by not meeting your need for stimulation. This may not be what you bargained for when you opened this book. Remember, I told you not to buy the book, and if you did to put it down. But since you are here, this clinical assessment is provided so that you can see how we can merge our bodies' experiences with welfare science, study, and intense observation.

Just When You Think You Grok It

The use of the Five Domains Model, like any tool, is inadequate by itself to help humans understand and care for others. However, its rigor helps us focus on others and hopefully rewire our brains to be more consciously and even subconsciously attuned to the welfare of others in ways that offer solutions to otherness. I have worked with parrots nearly my entire life, yet I still feel a deepening of my MI by using this model in parrot conservation.

The biggest shift I experienced was that I spent more time asking what the parrots would want when I assessed the welfare of ones under my care. I always thought that as a veterinarian I would naturally be assessing the welfare of an individual, but it turned out that I had a lot of room left to grow, even after thirty-seven years of working with free flying parrots. I still do now. I challenge myself to exert more energy watching the behavior of each individual bird and going through the Five Domains with emphasis on the mental component.

As it turns out, there seems to not be much I can do to improve the lives of the birds in our rescue centers who have experienced various injuries or poor growth during confiscation and rescue processes. We have limited resources in most locations, and our cages simply aren't big enough for the life of a parrot. In fact, no cage is big enough, as we say in our work. Nor can we provide the complex social and enrichment experiences these birds need in our projects' remote locations.

We adjust where we can, but the Five Domains Model slows me down to question my automatic and efficient procedures as an avian veterinarian, and make me aware of how far from ideal the welfare of birds caught in the wildlife trade is.. I always knew this, but by using the Five Domains I began to understand this more than before — in greater depth and, more recently, with increased anguish. Perhaps you, too, will experience discomfort as you grow your MI. But my growing awareness as I experienced the wildlife trade step-by-step helped me take the initiative to start a collaborative international movement (International Alliance for the Protection of Parrots) to reduce the demand for and stop the trade in parrots, and to do it with compassion not just for the birds but for people as well.

We've all made mistakes in applying MI to improve welfare and may continue to make hard or even tragic decisions. However overwhelmed we might feel when making changes to improve animal welfare, or the disassociation we may experience between our values and knowledge and our behavior, with the Five Domains Model we have more tools to enter into discussion with others so that together we make thoughtful, life affirming changes.

A Basis for Discussion

We continually cycle back to the limits of human language and senses to truly understand other beings. However limited our tools, we must strive to change our culture in a way that affirms the worth of every life. We could call these discussions, indeed our every movement shared with others, a process of ethical deliberation. Competent ethical discourse cannot be achieved by reading this book, nor the thousands of tomes dedicated to ethics. Ethical processes differ between cultures, and multicultural skills are an important part of moral reasoning, as is MI. It requires practice, hard work, and discomfort for our whole lives.

We can always improve. We are not static beings, nor are others, our communities, our science, or our medicine. Ethics cannot be achieved in just one period of focus. We are not alone in this life-long effort because ethical discourse cannot be done alone. It is a multidisciplinary effort that involves the community in which our care for birds is embedded. The question of what to do next is not what you or I do, but what we do together. By sharing this work, we help one another in our ethical practice and develop prosocial skills. Ethical practices are mentioned at the end of this chapter.

Prosocial and Antisocial Behaviors

Several species of birds exhibit prosocial behaviors, such as helping others. They also exhibit antisocial behaviors, such as harming others or undermining their wellbeing. The use of "prosocial" and "antisocial" is complicated when speaking about both humans and other animals. Antisocial in human terms is different in that it means an individual is against, unskilled at, or antagonistic toward human social interactions. We don't call humans antisocial if they are disinclined to engage in multispecies social interactions because by "social" we mean with our own species. In other animals, the use of these words is similar, as antisocial means not interacting well with your own species and prosocial means helping your own species. However, in this day and age when we are discovering so many multispecies interactions and our need to compensate for isolation and human exceptionalism, we appreciate that each species is not just in community with their own species. We all live in an interconnected web of relationships beyond any single species. For this reason, we will use prosocial and antisocial to mean interactions not just with conspecifics (same species), but also with heterospecifics (different species).

Besides defining prosociality as interacting with multiple species, considerations should be made in the use of this term. Any specific labels we give behaviors, such as cooperation, altruism, reciprocity, care, or compassion, may just muddy the waters as they invite humans to categorize at the risk of passing a moral judgement, even though many labels have a scientific basis. It's not that we don't want moral discussion, but categorizing behaviors as prosocial produces a layer that can interfere with growing our MI because moral discussion involves human cultural analysis about behavior. The MI invitation is to describe animal behavior without categorizing it either scientifically or morally, or even as prosocial or antisocial.

Let's take the example of a peregrine falcon. On a walk recently, my partner and I discussed how beautiful the falcons are and how they probably know it. "They are such jerks," we joked, knowing it was preposterous to equate ego and narcissism with this species just because they are so focused on hunting — and in the process, harming and killing. Yet projecting human qualities of "correct" and "incorrect" behavior is what we do to others all the time. Perhaps we don't consider peregrines as evil when they hunt and kill most birds, for that is their evolutionary niche, but what if it is a bird we study or are familiar with? It's hard for me to not see flashes of enemy images when a peregrine kills a parrot in our study area. We might imagine that from a parrot's point of view, the peregrine is certainly a jerk for killing others. At the same time, the nourishment from one dead parrot can feed the peregrine and her chicks, and thus the bird exhibits both prosocial (helping chicks) and antisocial (killing parrots) behaviors. Perhaps it's best to not even use the words "prosocial" or "antisocial." We might instead just describe the behavior.

The reason to eliminate labels that interpret an animal's behavior in terms of our human experience is to avoid engaging in dualistic thinking that can lead to a disconnect at best, and harm at worst because we see others as fundamentally flawed. Humans do this not just to other species but also to our own. The peregrine falcon in human terms is a "killer" and a "murderer." She "tortures" her victims by tearing their flesh before they are dead, and, "worse than that, she eats them." Such thought might lead humans to despise the bird and trap or hunt them to keep them from further killing.

Another example is the cowbird. I was birding with a friend when we saw a bird walking on the ground, and identifying her puzzled us for a while. "Oh, it's just a female cowbird," my friend said. She added, "I hate those birds." She explained she doesn't like them because a female cowbird will lay her eggs in the nest of another species, and those parents will raise her chicks, often to the detriment of their own chicks. I have heard other birders describe cowbirds as lazy and freeloaders, and even as if it being better if they did not exist at all.

We can lessen our judgement of this species by describing their behavior in scientific terms, such as brood or nest parasitism.. Even the relatively scientific word "parasite" has a negative human inference of someone who freeloads and takes advantage of another. Similarly, the words "harm" and "help" carry baggage. True, we do need scientific labels, but even these are subject to interpretation about what is really happening, and we can infuse value into our labels. For instance, "sexual coercion" is a label used to describe males forcing females to copulate with them. Even though it is a "scientific term," I think most of us cringe when we consider what it means.

Our discomfort though should not mean we shy away from discussing how behaviors harm individuals, but let's be specific as possible. We practice MI to diminish general terms that reinforce judgmental thoughts in order to see other individuals for who they are, be they human or not, and to analyze any harm that is occurring, Sometimes categorizing another animal's behavior is subtle, and we must be watchful of our thoughts and words.

Human Judgement Harms

An example of how human judgement can hurt another species is when I was working on a conservation team trying to help scarlet macaws in Central America. We inspected a nest that had three chicks, the youngest of which was much smaller than the other two. I suggested we keep checking on this chick to ensure its survival and supplement its care by climbing the tree or taking the chick into captivity. The local conservation team member replied, "No, we don't need to do that. Macaws are good parents. The mother takes care of her chicks, and she would never let one die." Well, the chick did die because we projected what we consider good human parenting onto a bird we love, which clouded our decision. On the other hand, the comment about parenting might have been a response to the fact that returning to climb this tree again would have been time and resource consuming, as the tree was deep in a forest that took a long drive and walk to get to.

Many other bird species are recipients of human judgement in terms of parenting, for better or worse, including the assumption that a bird's parents are automatons whose behavior is not worthy of observation. We can go to two extremes: one is to say that a behavior is conscious and then hold the animal culpable or praise them, and the other is to say that there is nothing subjective about their behavior worthy of our attention. In either case, we lose an opportunity to understand them and make better decisions. We do it to our own species, and we do it to others.

Even while writing this section, I see that I want to list all the prosocial behaviors I can think of so you will see birds as worthy others and not just as automatons. I am putting a premium on prosocial behavior among birds across species even if I couch it in terms such as displaying parenting, antipredator, cooperative breeding, and reciprocity behaviors; sharing food and foraging information; and leaders in flock formations working harder so that those behind them expend less energy.

To balance my preference for lifting up birds' prosocial behaviors, here are some antisocial and sometimes harmful behaviors in birds, so you understand people's knee-jerk reactions when judging other humans as well as other species. Birds harm and kill others of their same or other species (murder), kill their young (infanticide), eat their own species (cannibalism), mate outside their primary parenting bond (adultery), and exhibit sexual coercion (rape). How many crows have been shot because they are "evil?" Why have we misunderstood avian reproductive behavior by labeling their relationships as monogamous or "mated for life" when couplings with non-partners occur in species we previously considered "faithful"? Perhaps because we see them as we wish ourselves to be or not to be.

Practices at the end of this chapter use study and observation to help us approach our understanding of the world with as much multispecies competence as we can muster.

The First Step in MI

Given that there are over 10,000 species of birds, how can we even begin to discuss how to grow our MI with each one, let alone every one of the billion individual birds on the planet? Birds are so varied that it would take thousands of pages to highlight their senses, cognition, behavior, and welfare evaluations. Every year, more pages would have to be added to chronicle the uptick in research and observations.

To draw people into a practice of MI, I often concentrate on how birds, humans, and other mammals might be similar or different, but even then we need lifetimes of learning and observation. Lest you be overwhelmed, the first step in avian MI is to just put down this book and go watch a bird. Then pick up other books and resources and have conversations with other humans. We can learn a lot from each other.

To help get you started and to support avian MI, I can offer some spectacular recent observations of birds that usually astound people with whom I do bird walks and open up our perceptions of these species.

Flocking and Migrating Behavior

If possible, I lead walks where starlings move in murmurations. Starlings' murmurations form a synchronized cloud of movement over their roosting site, so whenever possible I look for where local starlings roost at night. If we are online in a seminar or indoors before a walk, I show one of the many online videos of starlings' coordinated flock movements. Amazingly, a flock may include hundreds to thousands of individuals, yet the group undulates as one. To see such a thing causes jaw-dropping wonder at their synchronization.

There are many theories about why they murmurate, including to confuse predators and share information. Many birds flying together may also conserve body heat. They may use sound and sight to synchronize their movements, both of which feed into their socially integrated proprioception system. This system helps them know where their body is and how it needs to move in relation to others.

Birds also move according to the placement of the stars, the moon, landscape markers, and Earth's magnetic field. The bar-tailed godwit has been tracked flying from North America to Australia — a distance of 8,400 miles — nonstop in 11 days. Specialized cells that sense Earth's magnetic field guide them when other clues are not available. Arctic terns will fly over 18,500 miles round-trip in one year along their migration route.

Cognitive Intelligence

Some birds that have been tested, most notably parrots, can outperform young children — and sometimes even university students — on intelligence and memory tests. Researchers found the intelligence of some species of parrots to be at the level of a four- to five-year-old human.[15] Crows can recall certain human faces and teach other crows to react defensively toward particular humans.[6] Cockatoos can choose a variety of tools in subsequent steps to help solve a problem that they have never faced before.[17]

Communication

Communication between individuals varies widely across species. Humans use both verbal and written communication, as well as bodily and facial movements. Other species use similar modes of communication but also different ones. Ants use pheromones, bees dance, and birds arrange their feathers in different patterns to relay information to one another. The kea parrot does not have external ears they can move like many mammals or bare facial patches that can display muscle movements as smiles and frowns, but they can use their eye movements and head feathers to indicate subjective states.[18]

In addition, many birds, like humans, are lifelong auditory learners and use calls to communicate. Corvids have particular calls that alert others to danger, its distance, and whether others should hide.[19,20] In one study, parrot parents were found to give names (signature calls) to their chicks, and the chicks learned the names of each of their parents.[21] In some species of birds the order of their calls reflects different meanings, which is called syntaxis.[22] Parrots are suspected to be able to do this, even when they use human language.[23] Alex, one of the most famously researched parrots, underwent extensive intelligence and language tests. On the night before he died, he said to his human companion and researcher Dr. Irene Pepperberg, "I love you. Be good."[24] It could be that he was repeating what she said, but Alex and other parrots in tests have used words they know in orders they had never heard before, yet corresponded to the particular context.

In their own language, parrots have dialects. A group of individuals that overnight at one roost site sounds different from another group at a nearby roost site. I have heard this in my own work as a parrot conservationist — particularly on Ometepe Island, Nicaragua, one of the few places where roost sites abound and are rather close together. At one roost site, I can hear how the birds sound different from those at other roost sites. I have also heard the differences between parrots that live higher in the mountains versus parrots that live along the Pacific coast of Guatemala. Unfortunately, there aren't many more parrot roosts on the heavily agriculturized lowlands in that country, so those dialects may be lost.

Culture

Even though a certain species may not be extinct, local extinction from a specific area results in losing not only the species' unique vocalizations but also its culture. In animals, a basic definition of culture is any behavior that is learned, shared, and persists over generations. For example, songbirds have dialects that are learned and passed down through generations.

Birds and Humans Together

All previous sections of the book have led up to this chapter, where we consider how birds are simultaneously so much like and unlike us, and how even comparing humans to birds defeats our purpose. We are enmeshed in a web of relationships with other species, a web with more than two nodes, and by no means is the human or the self the center node. Yet, try to convince our brains otherwise! Perhaps instead of fighting our human centeredness or experience, or seeking to change it, we can come to better understand it. There are many ways to do so.

We have reflected on how human culture is exquisitely intertwined with our relationships with birds, as is our biology, but this is an abstract theory. What is our direct experience around birds and their culture? To understand birds, we need to understand ourselves, and that is why we began this book with Emotional Intelligence (EI) and Social Intelligence (SI). Now let us delve deeper into our relationships with birds.

Ethno-ornithology in MI

Ethno-ornithology is the study of the relationship between humans and birds. It incorporates anthropological, cognitive, and linguistic approaches, as well as natural scientific observations to describe how humans perceive and value birds.

I took a course in this subject at the Religion and Nature Department at the University of Florida, and learned some aspects of this practice that help with developing MI. First, the person doing the observation is deeply embedded in the study, and their perceptions and projections are part of the analysis. We cannot study the relationship between other humans and birds without also looking at how we relate to all parties and our own observations. Second, we enter the observations with the intent to not judge how others perceive and value birds. We seek to understand their values and relationships to birds and describe the harm and benefit that emerge from this relationship. To be as nonjudgmental as possible, the description of harm and benefit uses our observational capabilities and the Five Domains Model. For instance, we might say that birds being held captive with chains around their ankles lowered their welfare status in several categories, such as by causing open abrasions and swelling on legs, instead of saying that people were cruel and ignorant of the harm they were causing.

In my informal ethno-ornithological studies on parrot conservationists in Central America, I learned the depth with which conservationists value their parrots, and that being on a team, sharing respect, and earning an income were among their most valued benefits of working with birds. Benefits also included experiencing love, beauty, physical challenges, and both interdependence and freedom, producing data, connecting to God and nature, having fun, being of service, and witnessing sacrifice. I also learned that trappers and poachers value their birds too.[25] The range of responses from both trappers and conservationists indicates we cannot say all trappers or all conservationists relate to birds in the same way. The ethnological approach led me to a way to grow my nonjudgmental observations while also witnessing harm and benefit as the consequences of humans' use and perceptions of birds.

Multispecies Intelligence and Culture

Early in my marriage to a bird novice, we went to the Bosque del Apache National Wildlife Reserve in New Mexico. I was preoccupied and worried I had asked him to spend too much time with birds, because we camped overnight, then drove around and frequently stopped to watch birds during the day.

One evening, we stopped at a shallow pond where sandhill cranes croaked in the late light. My spouse asked, "What are the darker ones? Are those another species?"

I didn't know he was watching that closely, but answered, "Those would be this year's young." He then grew so quiet that I thought he was bored and we should go. I turned away from the avian splendor and saw something even more wondrous: tracks of tears on his face. This in turn caused me to tear up.

Human emotions of awe and wonder are a part of EI and SI. They are mentioned here because the biology of emotions forms and informs our culture and hence the way humans relate to birds. Humans evolved to have these emotions, as well as disgust and fear, and other species can trigger such responses. Over time, language can wire our brains to react in ways that culture directs us to. Fears of snakes and spiders have an evolutionary origin. Our brains innately enable us to quickly identify objects like spiders or snakes, so that we quickly remove ourselves from danger. This inherited stress reaction that wires us to think these species are dangerous or disgusting can be unlearned. To truly see another species, we need to be aware of our evolved biology and how culture has sculpted it. In this way, we become ethno-ornithologists of our own behavior as well as others'.

Let's whomp some ethno-ornithology on my spouse. Why was he so moved by the family of cranes? And why was I moved in turn? Were those our innate responses to wonder and beauty? Yes. Is it culture telling us how astounding the cranes' parenting is, that they would fly for months over long distances with this year's chicks? Yes.

Once again, we witness nature versus nurture and biology versus culture, though like with other species both always have an influence. We are the lens through which the world enters our consciousness. The more adept we are in MI, the more likely we are to tenderly hold and reshape our lens to focus on others and see more clearly the beauty, worth, and dignity that surround us.

What Birds Mean to Humans

Defining what birds mean to humans is an ethno-ornithological pursuit to help us tell a story by unweaving the strands of our human culture interacting with other species, which when considered together, is known as bioculture. Entire books have been written about just one people's interaction in one part of the world with one or two species, and there is much more left to study and understand. We write our own stories, perhaps through journaling exercises as mentioned in the practices described previously in this book. We can also incorporate into those stories the everyday reactions we see when people interact with birds. By studying their reactions and values, as well as our own, we can settle into knowing how we see birds. Our bioculture will always keep us from truly understanding birds, for we would need to be the birds themselves to do so. But seeing birds as clearly as we can helps us lessen culture's hold on our thoughts and actions that may prove harmful to ourselves or birds. It also aids us in doing our part to grow a new culture, one based on the values of interdependence, beauty, and worth.

Shifting from Human-Centered Cultures

I have seen cultures develop within small groups of people who watch birds together over an extended period of time, mostly conservationists who monitor parrots together. We monitor them by counting them and studying their nests, flights, and foraging patterns. This intense focus on another changes us.

A veterinarian I know who worked with captive parrots told me once that something had changed within me because I had spent too much time with parrots in the wild. He was referring to how I am no longer able to work as a veterinarian with captive parrots. I cannot abide seeing them in cages, or with clipped wings, or unable to interface naturally with the complex social and environmental milieu from which they evolved. He said it was like I had become a parrot myself.

I have seen this same type of change among our conservation teams. Some of our parrot rangers began this work because they just needed a dependable job, or they were originally poachers who didn't want any trouble, so they went to work with the crazy conservationists. Then, all of a sudden, they became the most ardent and reverent conservationists themselves. This shared culture has also evolved among those who rescue parrots and provide sanctuary for them in North America. The camaraderie between sanctuary workers runs deep, and their common experience shapes them. As we share the work, we develop a parrot-centered culture that sees not just parrots as meriting our vigilance but all of life. This perspective diffuses out to the greater community, the children, and future generations. By watching birds, we change along with members of our groups, and this in turn changes the broader culture.

Love and Freedom

Earth's religions and philosophies can have a vison of a better society, and the idea that where we'd nearly all like to live is a place where we treat each other with love so that all are free. This is not a squishy love, but a love born of truly seeing the other and being supportive regardless. Unconditional solidarity is possible not just with humans but with all life. Freedom is not easily won, but we make space for others to experience freedom when we live not by society's constrictions that seek to harm some and benefit others, but in a society that promotes opportunities to flourish for everyone, no matter their fortunes of birth. Birds help us experience that love and freedom.

I worked with a man from Guatemala who was on a scarlet macaw conservation team. He had grown up in the days of the country's civil war where his father, like so many fathers, was killed. Before I truly knew him, I saw him as a tough, outdoorsy person who did not tolerate less than total seriousness. He was one of our tree climbers who had to spend long hours in the tops of trees, while the ground crew of technicians and veterinarians like me examined and measured the parrot chicks to log their health and development.

I once asked him what he thought about while he was up in the tree canopy under the direct tropical sun. He said, "I spend a lot of time looking out over the trees and at the macaws flying around, and down at you all working below. And I think, they cannot love the macaws as much as I do." I did not expect to hear this man use the word "love" about his relationship to parrots, but this sensibility is not unusual for those who work with other species. The birds change us, and in turn we can change the world.

In another project, I was collaborating with Indigenous parrot conservation teams in Guyana. I had trained a couple of villagers to do this work for a stipend so that the villages could lead their own conservation efforts. This meant that people who perhaps didn't think much about or spend much time with parrots were now spending most of their days with these birds. One much appreciated parrot species in Guyana is the sun parakeet. Their bright yellow and orange feathers can be seen and their squawks heard for miles as they fly high over the mountains on their daily routes. They are small, but they are mighty.

One Indigenous conservationist from another village came to help us with the annual parrot count. When asked what the sun parakeets meant to him, he said, "The parakeets are freedom. I need freedom." He echoed what is in so many people's hearts about birds. Perhaps our love is not just about the idea of freedom, but also our longing for wholeness and abundance, which each human bioculture has adapted to in its own way.

Seeing Birds Helps Us Help Them

Earlier, we discussed how seeing birds is good for human health. Recently, more studies have been published about how bird diversity and abundance impacts human health and satisfaction.[26-30] Watching birds, or even just listening to them — be it from outdoors or indoors — can result in long-lasting stress relief.[27] Mental wellbeing can be improved for up to eight hours after watching birds, and birdwatching can be more effective at increasing wellbeing and reducing stress than going for a walk. People with depression or other mental health conditions experienced significant improvements after watching our feathered friends. We evolved to be nourished by nature and to develop the hardwiring to be attracted to other species.

Paying attention to birds is also beneficial for our culture, especially if it is moderated by enhancing our MI and the intention for all beings to flourish. As we grow our awareness of others and of our connections to them, we also grow our shared interrelated health. However, we can't deeply see birds unless we do the work of understanding how our human filters have distorted who birds actually are or might be. To be good to ourselves, we need to be good to birds so that they are not diminished any more than they already have been. For the future we want to create, we have to consider birds and ourselves as clearly as possible. For this reason, it is important to know that all our natural intelligences are interconnected. For full Ecological Intelligence (EcI) we need to know humans and other species, and for MI we need to reach as full a level of Emotional Intelligence (EI) and Social Intelligence (SI) as possible. Interwoven in all of this is Spiritual Intelligence (SpI), and together the five intelligences are the tools that connect us to each and every other being on this planet.

Biology Enables Life, Culture Affirms Life: Parrots as an Example

Perhaps an example would serve us well to show how we can change human culture to further help other animals by experiencing other species for who they are. Birds in human culture have been a steady presence, so much so that Boria Sax in his book *Avian Illuminations* writes that humans would not be as we know ourselves without birds. We are, in some ways, indeed part bird. But what impact have our perceptions, values, and use of them had on birds?

Using ethno-ornithology focused on the past in the Americas, archeological evidence shows the trade of scarlet macaws reached from the area that is today Southern Mexico and Central America into Northern Mexico and the United States.[31] Evidence suggests the birds rarely lived past one year of age, and were often sacrificed to the gods as a way to petition for fertile growing seasons. They were also kept and even bred so that their feathers could be used in headdresses and other adornments. Scarring in bones suggests repeated live feather removal, a painful process if done before natural molting because the wing and tail feathers are deeply anchored in connecting tissues. Theories suggest that feathers were second only to jade in trade value in this part of the Americas.

Farther south, the parrot trade also flourished. Studies of parrot remains show that parrot species found normally only in the forests east of the Andes were discovered in human settlements further west.[32] Parrots were so highly prized that they were carried over the high mountains for long distances. These remains of many different parrot species show evidence of malnutrition and abuse, such as shorn beaks. We don't know how this trade impacted bird populations in the past, but we do know what is happening today.

The parrot trade is decimating parrots from the ecosystems in the Americas. Birds are no longer taken just over mountains or down rivers; they are shipped and smuggled all around the world to feed human desire. The reasons why humans desire parrots are for status symbols, their beauty, their ability to mimic and entertain, and companionship. Their sociality lends them to bonding with humans and being touched and cuddled, although many people aren't aware that most parrots will grow out of this behavior once they leave the chick or juvenile stage. The result of this desire for parrots has caused parrot populations to plummet globally, and also caused untold suffering of parrots who are harmed or killed during trapping and transporting. Those that survive are then relegated to captivity, where many fare no better than they did thousands of years ago in human communities. These complex social creatures are attuned to a quite different environment than a human home or cage.

Those who work in conservation teams protecting parrots have seen the decimating impacts of human desire on parrot populations as well as individuals harmed in the trade, and they want it to end. Others who work in parrot rescue and with the plethora of parrots who are abandoned or "unhomed" see how individual birds end up in crowded sanctuaries or, worse, have spent much of their lives experiencing the negative impacts of captivity. They, along with conservationists and those who have had parrots as pets, often become staunch proponents to end the trade and captivity of parrots.

They come to understand parrots to be much more than just victims of human desire, but truly beings with inherent worth and dignity. These long hours immersed in beauty and tragedy, significantly shifts their awareness. They are not alone, for what they come to know deeply about parrots is also bubbling up in the broader human cultures. Just as it was once not unusual to have chimpanzees and cetaceans in captivity, but now is considered harmful and morally suspect, the same cultural and legal shift is happening for parrots. Hopefully, one day this will end poaching, trade, and captivity, though it has been deeply embedded in the bioculture of many human cultures for a long time. Our biology sets the framework for who we are, but we can influence culture to affirm the worth and dignity of all.

Mourning as a Part of Culture

> *To live in this world, you must be able to do three things: to love what is mortal; to hold it against your bones knowing your own life depends on it; and, when the time comes to let it go, to let it go.*
> – Mary Oliver, "Blackwater Woods"[33]

As we travel toward the unknown of where MI leads us, there is no doubt that the journey will bring us both moments of blissful interconnection and heart-rending moments that may lead to weeks or years of anguish and bewilderment. I often say that my conservation work is like getting kicked in the gut on a daily basis. It seems never a day goes by that I don't hear how parrots have languished or been grievously injured or killed. The more I learn about parrots, the deeper the blade of awareness penetrates.

BIRDING FOR LIFE

Thank goodness there is the balance of healing that comes from connection, welcome, and love, not just for parrots but for the whole mess of existence. Each day, we fall in love with the view of a wild bird flying, for even in these small acts the sharp focus of evolution bedazzles. We see the light and experience the lightness, but the heavy burden of a biotic community must also be borne. We don't have to do so alone.

In sharing our despair or pain from knowing and loving birds, we too change the culture of those near and far. For instance, an indelible bond is formed among conservationists when we climb a parrot tree and realize that the chicks have been nabbed by poachers. In our conservation projects, we take time to share our feelings and values, and often this is at the base of a tree where a parrot family has been torn asunder. We then tell these stories to our families and friends, and in presentations, writing, and social media. By sharing our mournful responses to the loss, we shape our culture and our world.

We are not alone in mourning. For example, in the early 2000s the American crow population in North America was decimated by West Nile virus. The deaths impacted the birds who live in family groups in many ways.[34,35] Researchers found that at least one crow remained with each dying bird, and the birds also came together in novel ways. Crows with no relation to young birds assumed their care, and family flocks merged together. Surviving females joined other family units and helped them raise their babies. Adults who lost a mate moved back in with their parents. Crows didn't range as far as they had before the virus, and their foraging behavior was more conservative.

It was as if the crows were experiencing grief and, in many ways, mourned like us humans who reduce our engagement with the world while in our vulnerable states and rely mor on those around us. In times of lost relationships, new ones can be formed. We share our grief and come together in circles of mourning. We do this for ourselves and our kind, and we do it for others who need us to pay attention, to love, and to mourn.

Extinction Is Loneliness

> *Our bodies remember and our bodies know.*
> *Our bodies know what it feels like to be inside of a climax,*
> *vividly generative, overflowingly generous ecosystem. We know.*
> *We have all known the feeling of shattering loneliness.*
> *Extinction is loneliness. I can see it no other way.*
> — Alexa Firmenich[36]

The extinction of other species will leave humans as a sadder, reduced species as our community of relationships will have grown smaller. As grief must be borne, so must a lonelier future. Most of us have already experienced this, such as seeing fewer crows in the 2000s. Even most of our backyard birds are lower in numbers, and the diversity of those species has decreased. Perhaps it is time for the human culture to let loose the floodgates of tears about what has been lost. Our bodies and subconscious know deeply that something is amiss. By the time the loss reaches conscious thought, the deep wound is visible. If we can experience the loss of biodiversity as loneliness, we can perhaps change our culture that says humans drama has lasted long enough. We can change our ways to welcome others and be welcomed on Earth.

Even if we cannot forestall most of the dearth of life around us, we can know that we are never truly alone. Birds are seeing us and are in relationship with us. Crows know and remember human faces, and songbirds will move away from trails where humans travel. During the Covid-19 pandemic, the birds and other species came back into areas that humans had dominated. Life knows we are here. Even if we don't see them, they see us. It's time that we saw them, and the following practices will help us in this regard.

BIRDING FOR LIFE

Birding and Multispecies Practices

I believe building these connections with strange, baffling, or even discomfiting organisms is a practice of radical empathy you can try in your everyday life — offering openness, wonder, and care toward other creatures' incomprehensibility. When you encounter a life-form so unfamiliar that you find it uninteresting or repulsive, reach inward to find glimmers of resonance.

– Sabrina Imbler[37]

Remember while observing or interacting with birds that they have their own lives. They may be aware of and sense humans in a variety of ways that we cannot perceive. We may not be aware of our impact on them, but studies have shown that birds near human activity can be harmed.[38] Birds spend energy fleeing from trails, which results in lower egg weights and reduced chick health. For many species it is best to stay as far away as possible from birds.[38]

Practice 1: Understanding Animals With the Hokey Pokey

We can help ourselves and others grow our MI in a variety of ways, including through thoughts, conversation, action, and study. Often in our Nurture Nature programs at One Earth Conservation, we emphasize the use of our bodies with the intent of ratcheting down our thoughts, inner chatter, and projections. We do so to be present in the reality of what is before us in the moment, instead of a reality based on past experiences, our culture, and the stories our conscious mind fabricates to explain the world and our actions. Much of what motivates our behavior happens at a subconscious level, and our actions are underway before awareness reaches the thinking mind. We want to "listen" to what our bodies are doing. Humans process and sense the world not just in the mind, but throughout our bodies, such as through our senses and nervous system. We can also use our bodies to listen to what others are doing, saying, and needing. There is deep knowing in our shared evolution with other beings that developed all of our bodies with much in common, though we still have many differences as well.

One practice for using the body to grow MI is akin to the dance song, "The Hokey Pokey." The song begins with, "You put your left foot in, you put your left foot out, you put your left foot in, and you shake it all about. You do the Hokey Pokey, and you turn yourself around. That's what it's all about!" Each succeeding verse then has you put in a different body part until, in the last verse, "You put your whole body in, and that's what it is all about!"

In the MI form, we move various body parts in line with what another species is doing. We begin by imagining that we are another species. We can use our memory, view a video, or, even better, watch an actual individual. We closely observe what the other animal, or even plant, is doing, and we mimic that. Whatever their limbs are doing, we move our arms or legs like that — though some species such as corals might not have much external observable movement. Whatever the mouth or head is doing, we imitate the motions. What are the eyes, touch and taste receptors, ears, or nose doing and sensing? At some point, you are ready to put your whole body in motion (or no motion, depending on the species) to be that species.

If questioning thoughts arise, such as whether you are getting it right or if you look silly, let them go. This is not about getting it right. It is about celebrating and enjoying life. If this is done in a group or a circle outdoors, mirth abounds and spreads to spectators who cannot help but smile at a bunch of humans flapping their arms like wings.

People report after undertaking this practice, that they gain a deeper understanding of the species' motivations and behaviors that are often amazingly accurate. They also share that they didn't realize until they "became" the animal that other species had such complex motivations and behaviors. Through this exercise, people evolve to see that other beings indeed have subjective experiences, and that they aren't mere automatons responding to their environment. As with all MI practices, this embodied practice is followed up with study and reflection to check our human assumptions and increase our understanding.

Some versions of the Hokey Pokey end with people jumping in and out of the circle while singing, "Everyone in, everyone out." This practice helps us see that everyone is in our circle of concern for other species and remove human domination of our thoughts. They, us, and the world are so much more than we can ever imagine. We need to slow down to fathom life around us and commit ourselves to the pursuits of joy, wonder, awe, and beauty.

Practice 2: Interspecies Empathy – Being the Bird

This practice can be applied to any animal or plant species, and you can do the steps sequentially or even skip some. There are many variations in this exercise, and I invite you to develop your own to share with us. For instance, you may choose an animal with whom you empathize that you can see either in or outside your home. You can choose an animal that you know personally or see frequently. To challenge yourself, you might also choose an animal species or individual with whom you are unfamiliar, or with whom you experience uncomfortable feelings like strangeness, fear, irritation, or disgust.[34] Philosopher Timothy Morton proposes that the strangeness we sense in others reminds us that we are all interconnected and that, "Every life-form is familiar, since we are related to it."[5] Our relationship to each other goes deeper than our differences.

You may choose to go directly to step #5, the center and primary step of this exercise.

1. Think of an individual being. Write what you know about that being. What is the individual's species? Name? Gender? Age? Life stage (growing, juvenile, adult, etc.)? Health status? If you can't think of an individual you know, choose a species you would like to get to know better.
2. Observe them over a period of time, and write what you see them do. Explain what you see as if you were a reporter with

as little judgment or human projection as possible. In other words, don't try to interpret their behavior at this point. It may be easier to choose a short period of time or single behavior for this exercise, although you might find it useful for your relationship to journal about all the behaviors you encounter at some point.
3. Now guess what they are thinking and feeling related to their needs. What is their arousal level? It is high, medium, or low? Are they moving towards pleasure or away from discomfort? As a journal exercise, list your guesses.
4. To help you understand what you observed, do some research on the species regarding its behavior, communication, feelings, and thoughts.[39-49] You may find it difficult to find information about emotions and thinking in nonhuman species. Did you discover any new possible feelings or thoughts that might occur in this individual?
5. Now imagine that you are this animal. Wear their paws, scales, fur, or feathers for about fifteen minutes. Pick an animal that is in your home, yard, or along a walk or hike. You can also watch a video or nature documentary. Become them, and do what you observed them doing. As this animal, what are you thinking and feeling? For these fifteen minutes, just be them without analyzing too much why they do what they do. After you are finished, do a body scan. How did your body shift while being the animal? Ask yourself if you discovered anything new by pretending to be this animal. Share what you learned with another person and invite them into this journaling or imagination exercise.
6. To help you understand what you observed, do further research on their species regarding behavior, communication, feelings, and thoughts. Use the Five Domains Model as a guide to what another individual might be needing, and use the "Feelings" and "Needs" list in the Appendix to help you describe the feelings and needs of others. After researching, did you discover any new feelings or thoughts about the individual? If so, add them to your list.

7. Now, looking over the list of feelings and thoughts, make a list of this individual's needs. Try to be as complete as possible as you go through the behaviors observed or, if you have the time, spend a day as this individual. How might these needs be different from another individual of the same species, or from the average needs of this species?
8. What feelings and needs arise in you when you consider the feelings and needs of this individual?
9. What have you discovered about this individual, this species, yourself, or life through this exercise? If you have discovered anything, what needs of yours or this individual's were met or not met?
10. Go back and spend time connecting to the energy of this individual by reviewing their feelings and needs, and then do the same for yourself. Allow this to be a time of connecting to life without noisy thoughts, requests, or demands.
11. Now consider possible actions you might do or ask others to do based on this multispecies empathy exercise.
12. Share what you have learned or experienced with others and invite them into the exercise.

With humans, we have learned and evolved to do much of this exercise without much thought, though we all can improve our ability to understand what others are thinking. Courses and books abound on how to read facial and body language, or on how to take the perspective of another by imagining you are them, which was covered in the SI chapter. In *Mindwise*, Nicholas Epley determined that the superior way to understand another is to just ask them. Yes, they may be making up a story about why they did something, but at least it is them making up the story and not you. We pay attention to birds so that we understand their stories from their point of view.

Practice 3: Being a Bird for Five Seconds at a Time

The previous practices are for focusing on certain species that you wish to acquire more empathy and understanding for. This can be done in a much shorter time, such as when you are occupied with other pursuits. In this case, any time you see a bird, breathe deep and move like the bird. Perhaps you will wave your hands as if flying, hop along the ground, or simply move your head or eyes as they do. You can also try to imitate their sounds.

In places where my spouse and I walk, we hear fish crows that have a more nasal caw than the American crow. When we hear them calling, we — well okay, maybe I more than he — begin emitting nasal honks, sometimes during the entire walk. It's good that not many people are within listening distance of us. If I think I might be embarrassed or am in a group where my actions or sounds might be disturbing to birds or humans, I minimize my movements and sounds. By moving our bodies in synch with another, it is as if we are sharing a ritual with them, and are on the same team undertaking a common endeavor that connects and binds us to another species.

Practice 4: A Conversation With Birds

In the case of other species, there are limits to any exercise we can do to understand them, since we barely can do so with our own species. Even asking another human for information to better understand them has restrictions, because our conscious selves make up stories about why we do certain things or think a certain way. And we cannot ask a bird what is going on for them. Or can we?

In this practice, we imagine that a bird could respond to us. Indeed, upon close observation you might be able to see that the bird is reacting to you, perhaps by moving a certain way or changing their behavior. Choose a distance between yourself and the bird that will not disturb them. We have a data collecting form we use in parrot conservation on which we record the behavior of observed birds before we think they are aware of us, after they are aware of us, and as we approach them. We do this for their welfare so that we know a good distance from which to monitor our birds and nests without harming them by reducing nest attentiveness or making them use their energy output to evade us.

Beyond a scientific and close observation, we can also greet birds in our own way and talk to them. I do this when coming across a bird I see or hear. I may say, "Oh, hello there," with a curious tone to my voice. I might also call them by name, such as, "Hello, raven. What are you doing?" I say this more to attune myself to them, and perhaps my tone of voice and familiarity conveys information to which they respond. But mostly I do this because I want to "talk to the animals."

Besides developing an intuitive connection with other beings, I find speaking to them opens me up to a spaciousness where I am curious and aware of them. It orients my body to perceive and focus on them and gain new knowledge and understanding not only of them but of their world. Try it yourself with the following guidelines:

1. Begin by turning your body towards a bird you see or hear. Breathe deeply if you can.
2. Then greet them in a friendly and casual manner such as, "Good morning. How are you?" Perhaps a simple "Hello" will suffice.
3. Then ask them one or more of the following questions: "What are you doing? What are you feeling and needing? Why did you just do that?"
4. You might then ask if there is anything you can do for them. For instance, you might hear a bird call when you approach them. You might ask, "What did you say? Do you want more space around your nest?"

I am frequently out counting parrots and watching them fly near me, or over me. They often tilt their heads to look down at me and sometimes call out. I ask them, "What do you think of me? Do you wish I wasn't here? Are you afraid of me or mad at me?" Some parrots will divert their direction of flight so they don't fly right over me, while others circle back around as if giving me a second look. While part of me is analyzing this behavior, I also talk to them, even aloud at the risk of disdain from my colleagues. "Why did you come back? What are you thinking? Why don't you fly over me? Have you been shot at or predated by others like me? Is there anything I can do to repair the harm that has been done?"

My conversation with wild parrots takes on a sense of urgency when I am near a parrot nest, or when we are climbing a tree to confirm if it has an active nest and ascertain the health status of potential eggs or chicks. Sometimes, the parents are in the area. They will call out and even circle the tree multiple times while vocalizing loudly, which we interpret as distress. While juggling the needs of the conservation team, I also focus on the birds. I talk to them rather continuously, asking forgiveness and explaining what we are doing.

When I was much younger and working in Guatemala during the civil war, the yellow-naped parrots were subjected to nearly 100% poaching of their nests. So frequent were my conversations with the parrots that when I was near their nests, a little song emerged. It began, "Oh, mama. You don't have to be afraid. I'm just a passin' by." I didn't want to disturb the birds or, even more so, be associated with those of my kind that would harm them.

I converse with birds so that I can use my human sense of language to mold my brain into focusing on a non-human. I also do so to set an example to other humans that together we can see birds not as objects without any relationship to us, but as worthy subjects with whom we are in a most profound relationship.

Practice 5: Silly Walks

In a previous practice, I mentioned how I talk to animals I encounter. It just seems like a polite thing to do, and the urge to speak to them arises spontaneously. On the surface this may appear silly, but can we really have too much silliness? At the same time, interacting with other species fosters respect for others. It helps me focus on their inherent worth and dignity, as well as their behavior. I also imitate their sounds and sometimes move like them. And if they are ill, I will rescue them if I think it is in their best interest. If they are dead, I move them to a guarded location, bow, and say a little prayer.

If you encounter me on my daily walk and avert your eyes or stare, you wouldn't be the first. One time I was ambling along our neighborhood streets and came across a groundhog that had been hit by car and was a squishy mess. I came up to her and said, "I'm sorry." Then, I started looking for a way to move her out of the middle of the road. I saw a group of adults and young girls a few blocks up and knew I was exhibiting unusual behavior in front of strangers. Stare they did as I found sticks and leaves to move the animal to some bushes on the side of the road. Because I had an accidental audience, my bow was briefer than usual.

As I approached the humans, they stopped their activity and stared at me. One mother said, "I am so glad you did that. I wanted to but just didn't know how to go about it. You set a great example for the girls." In your MI practices, go ahead and take risks as you respect the beauty that life is. So be silly, as your silliness might just save Earth.

Practice 6: Bird Stories and Meditations

Resources are available to help guide us to understand other species.[39-49] Some scientific writing can help us interpret the behavior of others and gain a greater understanding of their daily lives. This writing can also be told in story form, such as novels, films, poems, children's books, and meditations.[50] One such resource is the children's book by Gail Koelln, *What Would the Parrot Say?*, published by our organization. It imagines what a scarlet macaw says about being caged or trapped. The book ends with information about parrots and what you can do to help.

We have also produced a guided meditation video that helps us understand the life of a scarlet macaw.[51] While being anthropomorphic in style, the story is based upon thousands of hours of observing parrots. We developed this video to share what is known about parrots, because not everyone has the opportunity to study and reflect on a parrot's life. Other guided meditations also exist to help us, including one I created with a gopher tortoise.[51]

Practice 7: Community Ethical Practices

The practice of honing our ethical skills and aligning our thinking with our actions that care for ourselves and others is not a solitary effort. It is a conversational method that, in the Western world, was first developed by Socrates with his students. This was later named the Socratic Method, which consists of dialogue between a teacher and students. The teacher continually probes the students with questions that expose their underlying beliefs. For nearly 2,500 years teachers have used this method, often formalizing the method in classroom situations called Socratic Discussions, for which the teacher raises a question and the students respond.

Other practices do not rely on a teacher leading or students responding to the teacher's questions but rely on students interacting with each other. These are communitarian ethics, as opposed to principled ethics, in that there are no guiding rules or reliance on consistency of thought but only interactions between two or more individuals. For a more in-depth understanding of both principled and communitarian ethics, read my article about wildlife ethics.[52] No matter which ethical approach you choose, these following guidelines will aid your process:

1. Remind people that this is voluntary and that they may disengage at any time.
2. Remind people of the need for deep listening, which involves letting people speak without interruption.

3. Invite people to breathe deeply at the beginning of the practice and throughout. Also, invite people to undertake a variety of bodily movements as discussed in earlier exercises, such as spreading out your hands, looking up and out, and bowing. This sets up the body for an openness to connection.
4. Invite people to remember a pleasant experience or a time when they felt seen and heard. This too sets up the body for openness to connection.
5. Explain the process thoroughly and give a brief demonstration.
6. Allow ample time, both during and afterwards, for people to share their practice experience.
7. After the practice, ask people what they experienced and felt, as well as what they learned and were challenged by or grateful for.
8. Consider forming a regular group that can practice these exercises and grow in capacity to take on increasingly challenging subjects.

Narrative Ethics

In narrative ethics, stories are told about ethical choices. The speaker clarifies their own needs and values, as do the listeners. They also highlight moral guidance to living a good life, not just in care, but in multispecies relationships and all other aspects of one's life. These narratives of witness, with their experiential truth and passion, compel re-examination of accepted practices and ethical precepts. This allows us as a community to develop our ethical abilities. Using narrative ethics that emphasize communication does not preclude the use of principled ethics. Indeed, both contribute to understanding moral life and the process of ethical decision making.

Let's take the case of a bird striking a home's window. The characteristics of glass can fool a bird into thinking a clear flight path exists through a window, but instead the bird is injured or killed. An estimated one billion birds die every year in the United States from collisions with windows, and recent studies suggest that this may be an underestimation.[53] What should a homeowner, business owner, or government authority do? How much effort should they put into the many different preventative measures that decrease bird strikes on windows? There is no "right" or "wrong" ethical philosophy or principle here to determine. Instead, the process brings together everyday humans struggling to make the best choices possible in any given situation.

People might tell stories about seeing hundreds of birds' still bodies on an urban sidewalk next to a skyscraper that was illuminated at night when bird deaths are frequent. In the process of telling, an internal dynamic occurs within both the teller and listeners that stimulates emotions as well as conscious and subconscious thought of past experiences, values, and cultural constructs. This dynamic helps us align our behavior with our thoughts and emotions.

Transformational Reasoning

Transformational reasoning occurs when one internalizes and clearly articulates the thoughts, arguments, or position of another. This occurs because one's reasoning has integrated with another's. We begin with the presentation of controversial situations involving birds, and then participants take turns arguing various viewpoints. A prime example would be the situation of cats — domestic, abandoned, and feral — being allowed outdoors. Over two billion birds in the United States alone are killed by cats every year.[53] If ever there is a controversial topic, this is it. The most volatile reaction I ever received from a sermon I delivered was after I included a story of cats hunting wildlife and what to do about it. I have also used this topic when inviting veterinary students into a transformational reasoning process, and the room generally erupts with passionate arguments, derailing the intention of the practice itself.

This approach to community ethical formation requires spaciousness and structure to help people navigate its provocative invitation to engage in controversial subjects and temporarily take on the views of others. It is important to repeat what one has heard and argue for the case you don't agree with. In this process of pretending to take the other side, one gains an empathy for other positions and grows in sophistication with one's newly acquired and more integrated ethical approaches. Participants can also be urged to build a consensus regarding the issue to further expand their abilities in discourse.

Needs-Based Ethics and Compassionate Communication

Compassionate communication, based on Marshall Rosenberg's Nonviolent Communication (NVC) theory, emphasizes honesty and empathy in interpersonal and intrapersonal relationships.[54] NVC is based on the understanding that human beings operate best in social groups when they receive empathy. Through practice, NVC leads to shifts in thinking and emotional responses. Greater connection and rapport between individuals are paramount in social discourse and occur if more conscious verbal and body language are employed. Connection is founded on the idea of universal needs and not on judgment, blame, or domination to meet those needs. Instead, empathy through deep listening, authentic sharing of needs and feelings, and clear requests are the best strategies for forming creative solutions so that everyone is heard and the needs of everyone, including nonhuman animals, are considered. By engaging in compassionate communication, people can meet needs, which produces positive emotions and commitment. In the case of outdoor cats and wildlife, we seek to empathize with the needs of everyone involved in the case:

- the injured or killed bird
- the bird's chicks, mate, or flock mates
- the particular bird species

- the cat
- those that interact with the cat and have a relationship with the cat (humans, other cats, other species)
- any veterinarian or veterinary team members
- family members of those working with the bird
- people who find the bird
- people who care for cats who attack a bird
- habitats and other species that evolve in balance with the bird (as prey and predators)
- individuals within local conservation and wildlife groups
- birdwatchers
- members of animal welfare groups
- future generations of children
- yourself as a reader

By equally considering the needs of all involved, we can generate creative, synergetic solutions that deliver the best care possible to the broadest constituency. Keeping all needs on the table allows us to break free from ideological stances or cultural constructs that might normally restrain us, such as animal rights versus animal welfare, or domination versus mutualism. Instead, we come into a space to hear one another, and to listen to how life reverberates through the species in our communities. This does not ensure that hard choices won't still be necessary. Even if our choices are regrettable, such as euthanasia or trapping feral cats to live in a preserve, our work is sustained by connecting fully to the broad diversity of life around us.

Practice 8: More Ethno-ornithology Practices

Ethno-ornithology practice takes place wherever we observe other people, even while taking part in an activity or situation in which others are involved. The ideal place would be a bird watching event, such as a bird walk or tour. Other examples would be attending a presentation on birds, a club of birders, a nature group, or a shared experience using media such as books, songs, or films.

This practice can take place whenever we are embedded in a social situation where we can reflect on people's relationships to birds or other species. In some cases, birds might not be the focus, and the absence of mentioning birds may indicate how people relate to and value them.

For instance, we might attend a religious event such as a congregational service, and observe if, how, and where other species are mentioned. As a Unitarian Universalist minister, I constantly note during Sunday morning services if other species are mentioned. The lack of nonhuman references could indicate a different value system than mine, but I cannot be sure, for while I ponder about others, I ponder about myself. My goal is not to concentrate on what the differences may be, for this might engender judgment, but what value systems are present and how they impact me and others.

While I study others, I am also studying myself. This is a hallmark of an ethno-ornithology practice: we are both the researcher and the subject. Such a practice might lead to changes in community expectations and values, especially when undertaken with compassion and intention.

For years I shared my ethno-ornithology observations with my spouse, another Unitarian Universalist minister. I would let him know after a service led by him or others how many times they incorporated or overlooked another species, and how I experienced that inclusion or exclusion. For instance, in a prayer other ministers might mention those lost during a recent flood or the results of climate change, but they would mention only human lives and suffering. Their leadership, with inclusion of other beings or lack thereof, signals to other people how we might relate to and value more than the human world.

By sharing my experience, often not as nonjudgmentally as is the ethno-ornithological ideal, my spouse has begun to incorporate more nonhuman reference points. For instance, when a Sunday service begins, Unitarian Universalists will often sound a bell or chime. In one of his congregations, they began the service with "Bell and Bird," a video of someone sounding a bell along with a vocalizing bird.[55] He now also includes more nonhuman animals in prayers, songs, readings, and sermons, though rarely to the extent that my desire for true decentering of humans is reflected.

Having navigated a divergence between myself and others in terms of avian value, in both the intimate realms of marriage and shared religious life as well as in the world of parrot conversation, I offer some guidelines on ethno-ornithological practice.

1. Attempt to orient yourself as both a nonjudgmental observer and a subject of observation.
2. Take note of your observations and thoughts with the intention of seeing how the ways that others view and use birds are not wrong, though their values, thoughts, and uses may differ from yours.
3. Include how your observations may have been formed in a dominant culture or seen from a demographic normally viewed as the oppressor (or oppressed) and that to describe another culture without being part of it is fraught with multicultural banana peels. It is so easy to slip up! This entire practice involves your inner discourse of how you filter what you experience and observe.
4. Write down — or if you prefer, audio or video record — what you observe during conversations and actions you witness.
5. What is your response to what you witnessed?
6. Make notes in the margin of your text or highlight in some other fashion the various values, words, or usages regarding birds.
7. Are there any trends or patterns that you are observing? Do some focuses appear more often than others? What have you learned?
8. Summarize your results as if you are a peaceful alien species who is in awe of humankind. Report on how you experienced humanity in this situation. What is the human culture you witnessed regarding the traditions and practices with birds, and how do humans relate to birds?

9. Consider how your experience could be shared with others in a curious and compassionate manner. What more can you learn from and experience through this sharing? How do others experience their values, thoughts, and usages of birds?
10. You might also incorporate specific questions in an interview format to learn more explicitly about others' relationships with birds.
11. How can what you've learned about another culture help inform multicultural conservation teams in their approaches to working with local communities and varying demographics?

A shortened version of this practice consists of just one or two questions to ask or themes to pursue when you interact with other people. For instance, you might ask if anyone has birds in their home and why they have them. You could also ask if people make time to observe birds and, if so, what they feel and think when they are birding. If you feel especially brave, you might ask if people treat different species of birds differently, such as eating or hunting certain species while protecting others. I'd suggest *not* doing this in the United States around the Thanksgiving holiday.

One of the biggest benefits of this practice is working with and relating to people to achieve increased welfare for all concerned. For instance, over the years I have experienced the lives of hunters, poachers, traders, and buyers, as well as consumers of wild parrots for food, adornment, income, pets, prestige, company, and a variety of other values. When using this practice, I find that I have less judgement of them and more skill in listening to them and appreciating our cultural differences. This goes a long way in not only working together as teams of people who learn from each other, but also in gaining the resilience needed to see the wonder and growth possible within every human and avian encounter.

Notes

1. Regan T. *The Case for Animal Rights*. University of California Press: Oakland, CA. 2004.
2. Kornfield J. *A Path with Heart: A Guide Through the Perils and Promises of Spiritual Life*. Bantam Books: New York, NY. 2009.
3. Brooks D. Is self-awareness a mirage? *New York Times*. Last modified September 16, 2021. https://www.nytimes.com/2021/09/16/opinion/psychology-consciousness-behavior.html
4. De Waal F. The brains of the animal kingdom. *Wall Street Journal*. Last modified March 22, 2013. https://www.wsj.com/articles/SB10001424127887323869604578370574285382756
5. Morton T. *Humankind: Solidarity with Non-Human People*. Verso Books: New York, NY. 2017.
6. Aiyer K. The great oxidation event: How cyanobacteria changed life. *American Society of Microbiology*. Last modified February 18, 2022. https://asm.org/articles/2022/february/the-great-oxidation-event-how-cyanobacteria-change
7. Matthew S, et al. Enhanced terrestrial nutrient release during the Devonian emergence and expansion of forests: Evidence from lacustrine phosphorus and geochemical records. GSA Bulletin 135(7-8). 2022. https://doi.org/10.1130/B36384.1
8. Barrett LF. *How Emotions are Made*. Pan Books: Clerkenwell, London. 2018.
9. Yong E. *An Immense World: How Animal Senses Reveal the Hidden Realms Around Us*. Random House: New York, NY. 2022.
10. Pascal F, et al. Anxiety-like behavior in crayfish is controlled by serotonin. *Science* 344. 2014. https://www.science.org/doi/10.1126/science.1248811
11. Even N, et al. General stress responses in the honey bee. *Insects* 3(4). 2012. https://pmc.ncbi.nlm.nih.gov/articles/PMC4553576/
12. How much time do you spend looking for your car keys? *Keys 4 Cars*. Last modified February 8, 2021. https://keys-4-cars.com/time-spent-looking/

13. Mellor D, et al. The 2020 five domains model: Including human-animal interactions in assessments of animal welfare. *Animals* 10(10). 2020. https://pmc.ncbi.nlm.nih.gov/articles/PMC7602120/
14. Joyner L, et al. Guide to Understanding and Reducing Harm to Parrots in Suriname. One Earth Conservation. Accessed November 21, 2024. https://www.oneearthconservation.org/_files/ugd/d204d4_309fef0f70d4496893889975bc30b257.pdf
15. Pepperberg IM, et al. Logical reasoning by a Grey parrot? A case study of the disjunctive syllogism. *Behaviour*, 156(5-8). 2019. https://doi.org/10.1163/1568539X-00003528
16. Marzluff JM, et al. Lasting recognition of threatening people by wild American crows. *Animal Behaviour* 79(3). 2010. https://doi.org/10.1016/j.anbehav.2009.12.022
17. Auersperg A, et al. Spontaneous innovation in tool manufacture and use in a Goffin's cockatoo. *Current Biology* 22(21). 2012.
18. Diamond J, et al. *Kea, Bird of Paradox: The Evolution and Behavior of a New Zealand Parrot*. University of California Press: Oakland, CA. 1999.
19. Marzluff J, et al. *Gifts of the Crow*. Simon and Schuster: New York, NY. 2012.
20. Mates EA, et al. Acoustic profiling in a complexly social species, the American crow: caws encode information on caller sex, identity, and behavioural context. *Bioacoustics* 24(1). 2015.
21. Berg KS, et al. Vertical transmission of learned signatures in a wild parrot. *Proc. R. Soc. B.*279 585–59. 2011. http://doi.org/10.1098/rspb.2011.0932
22. Suzuki TN, et al. Experimental evidence for compositional syntax in bird calls. *Nature Communications* 7 (10986). 2016. https://doi.org/10.1038/ncomms10986
23. Roubalová T, et al. Comparing the productive vocabularies of grey parrots (*Psittacus erithacus*) and young children. *Anim Cogn* 27(1). https://pmc.ncbi.nlm.nih.gov/articles/PMC11196360
24. Carey B. Brainy Parrot Dies, Emotive to the End. *New York Times*. Last modified September 11, 2007. https://www.nytimes.com/2007/09/11/science/11parrot.html

25. Joyner L. Needs of poachers and conservationists. One Earth Conservation. Last modified May 30, 2017. https://www.oneearthconservation.org/post/2017/05/30/needs-of-poachers-and-conservationists
26. Camacho-Guzmán A, et al. Connectedness to Nature, Wellbeing and Presence of Birds. *Fronteiras* 12(1). 2023. https://orcid.org/0000-0003-3328-3919
27. Hammoud R, et al. Smartphone-based ecological momentary assessment reveals mental health benefits of birdlife. *Scientific Reports* 12. 2022. Accessed November 21, 2024. https://doi.org/10.1038/s41598-022-20207-6
28. Haupt A. Birdwatching has big mental-health benefits. Here's how to start. *Time Magazine.* November 14, 2022. https://time.com/6231886/birdwatching-mental-health/
29. Randler C. Committed bird-watchers gain greater psychological restorative benefits compared to those less committed regardless of expertise. *Ecopsychology* 14(2). https://www.liebertpub.com/doi/10.1089/eco.2021.0062
30. Zieris S, Kals E. Nature experience and wellbeing: Bird watching as an intervention in nursing homes to maintain cognitive resources, mobility, and biopsychosocial health. *Journal of Environmental Psychology* 91. 2023. https://doi.org/10.1016/j.jenvp.2023.102139
31. Schwartz C. Scarlet macaws, long distance exchange, and placemaking in the U.S. Southwest and Mexican Northwest, ca 900-1450. Accessed November 21, 2024. https://d1rbsgppyrdqq4.cloudfront.net/s3fs-public/c7/224653/Schwartz_asu_0010E_19945.pdf
32. Capriles JM, et al. Pre-Columbian transregional captive rearing of Amazonian parrots in the Atacama Desert, *Proc. Natl. Acad. Sci.* 118(15). 2021. https://doi.org/10.1073/pnas.2020020118
33. Oliver M. Blackwater woods. In *American Primitive*. Backbay Books: New York, NY. 1983.
34. Erickson L. West Nile virus: Crows dealing with grief. Laura Erickson's for the Birds. Last modified October 7, 2004. https://www.lauraerickson.com/radio/program/10740/west-nile-virus-crows-dealing-with-grief/

35. Clark AB, et al. Effects of West Nile virus mortality on social structure of an American Crow (*Corvus brachyrhynchos*) population in upstate New York. *Ornithological Monographs* 60. 2006. https://doi.org/10.2307/40166828.
36. Firmenich A. Extinction is Loneliness. The dark mountain project. Accessed April 15, 2023. https://dark-mountain.net/extinction-is-loneliness/
37. Imbler S. Are you really so different from the blue sea glob? *New York Times* November 24, 2022. https://www.nytimes.com/2022/11/24/opinion/sea-creatures-blue-blob.html
38. Livezey KB, et al. Database of bird flight initiation distances to assist in estimating effects from human disturbance and delineating buffer areas. *Journal of Fish and Wildlife Management* 7(1). 2016. https://doi.org/10.3996/082015-JFWM-078
39. Ackerman J. *The Genius of Birds*. Penguin Press: New York, NY. 2016.
40. Bekoff M. *The Emotional Lives of Animals: A Leading Scientist Explores Animal Joy, Sorrow, and Empathy - and Why They Matter*. New World Library: Novato, CA. 2007.
41. Bekoff M, Pierce J. *Wild Justice: The Moral Lives of Animals*. The University of Chicago Press: Chicago, IL. 2010.
42. Bond AB, Diamond J. *Thinking Like a Parrot: Perspectives from the Wild*. The University of Chicago Press: Chicago, IL. 2021.
43. De Waal F. *Mama's Last Hug: Animal Emotions and What They Tell Us about Ourselves*. W. W. Norton & Company: New York, NY. 2020.
44. Emery N. *Bird Brain: An Exploration of Avian Intelligence*. Princeton University Press: Princeton, NY. 2016.
45. Gruen L. *Entangled Empathy: An Alternative Ethic for Our Relationships with Animals*. Lantern Publishing & Media: Woodstock, NY. 2015.
46. Higgins J. *Sentient: How Animals Illuminate the Wonder of Our Human Senses*. Atria Books: New York, NY. 2022.
47. Masson J, McCarthy S. *When Elephants Weep: The Emotional Lives of Animals*. Delacorte Press: New York, NY. 1995.
48. Martinho-Truswell A. *The Parrot in the Mirror: How evolving to be like birds makes us human*. Oxford Press: Oxford, UK. 2022.
49. Safina C. *Beyond Words: What Animals Think and Feel*. Henry Holt & Company: New York, NY. 2015.

50. Animal meditations. Season Four. Accessed November 21, 2024. http://www.animalmeditations.com/
51. Nurture Nature Practices. *One Earth Conservation*. Accessed November 21, 2024. https://www.youtube.com/playlist?list=PLT3f4GhFgYKjHF81crbzwcBFYN814IiEM
52. Joyner L. Ethical considerations in wildlife medicine. *Wildlife Rehabilitation Bulletin* 39(1). 2021. https://nwrajournal.online/index.php/bulletin/article/view/248
53. New study confirms building collisions kill over one billion birds annually in U.S. American Bird Conservancy. Last modified August 7, 2024. https://abcbirds.org/news/bird-building-collisions-study-2024/
54. Rosenberg M. *Nonviolent Communication. A Language of Life*. Puddle Dancer Press: Encinitas, CA. 2015.
55. Bell and Bird. One Earth Conservation. Accessed November 18, 2024. https://youtube.com/playlist?list=PLT3f4GhFgYKhpINioud_nbGj4Q3HGPgwz&si=CxHQBBHBw6hLGT6U

Ecological Intelligence
Holy Bird Shit!

Ecological intelligence is not speech. It is an act. It is an act of weaving and unweaving our reflections of ourselves on Earth, of scattering eyes upon it, and of scattering the Earth upon our eyes. It comes alive between yes and no, between what is and what is not, between science and non-science. And as soon as it becomes acquisitive, something egotistic ... it vanishes.

– Ian McCallum[1]

What Is Ecological Intelligence?

Ecological intelligence (EcI) is the capacity to recognize the often-hidden web of connections between human activity and nature's systems, as well as the subtle complexities of their intersections, to minimize harm and maximize benefit for all. It is both an intellectual and an emotional expertise that strives to nourish others and ourselves; caring for one is caring for all. If emotional, social, and multispecies intelligences mean being open to the feelings and needs of others, then EcI is the awareness of how the feelings and needs of all others interact in the complex ecology of the web of life.

Life may feel at times like a sticky mess when our allegiances are torn between ourselves and others. The reality of life, however, is that it often consists of more harmony than cacophony. In some ways, our lives cannot help but sing in harmony — we can't help but play our part in the drama of nature that eons of evolution granted us. Often, though, it is a challenge to hear the harmonic subtleties and add our voices in a way that consciously supports the entire vast choir of existence. This is why we practice and nurture our EcI for the flourishing of all.

A Community of Relationships

There are multiple ways in which our lives are held together by the web of life. The elemental atoms within us come from the big bang that formed the first stars. Much later, when the dust of stars coalesced into Earth, carbon, hydrogen, nitrogen, and oxygen arranged themselves into molecules. These molecules, such as water, first produced primordial seas, and then were processed through towering conifers, dinosaur blood, and the first great ape tears to become you.

We breathe in oxygen that was once part of the bodies of fish, birds, and early hominids such as *Homo erectus*, and they become us. We exist because of those who lived before us and those still living among us.

If we pause to consider our place in life, it is clear that humans belong on this planet. Earth comes out of stardust, oceans come out of Earth, Africa comes out of the oceans, and we come out of Africa. We are well versed to be full members of the universe. We also know through physics and ecology that we are inextricably interconnected to all of life and that our existence depends on others' and Earth's processes. However, we live in a constant state of forgetfulness, and many cultural practices seek to wipe clean any memory of interdependence and replace it with separation so that we do not feel welcome and do not welcome others into a flourishing life. For this reason, we need to hone our awareness of reality through the practice of Ecological Intelligence (EcI). Birding is one such EcI practice and is among the most enjoyable and available practices.

EcI Is Awareness of Interconnecting Harm

By paying attention to birds, we discover the often hidden interconnections of interdependent maleficence. Once we train ourselves to do this, we realize that birds near and far are in trouble. Species are declining at alarming rates, and climate change produces extra stressors and challenges to which we are unsure if birds can adapt.

One goal of birding is not to experience shame, but to gain awareness about the mesh of interdependent maleficence in which we all are stuck. Interdependent maleficence is when an action or set of behaviors leads to a chain of harm that echoes through the lives of many individuals.

It may be hard for humans to recognize examples of harmful ecological behavior outside of our own actions, given our propensity to romanticize the concept of ecological balance and denigrate our own species. We tend to think that whatever one species does to harm another one contributes to the flourishing of a habitat. But what other species do can also knock things out of balance.

In reality, there is no such thing as ecological balance. Yes, there are fairly tightly woven pockets of interaction and interdependence, but these are always being rewoven as species and the planet evolve. In general, scientists know that ecosystems are more of a spiral or a wave, never in total balance but always changing. Life came and went long before humans came into being; an estimated 99.9% of all species that ever existed are now extinct.

Cats and Maleficence

I once saw a sign in a bar that said, "Do not leave your drink unattended. The cat is an asshole." Though funny, this is a projection of human judgment on a cat's motivations and might even besmirch their inherent worth and dignity. In the section that follows, we talk about a web of harm entwining cat companions. This in no way is meant to cast aspersions on this species or on the humans involved with them. Indeed, with the complex interplay of multispecies relationships, our goal is to become aware of the consequences of our actions, the interacting needs within the biotic community, and where we can reduce harm.

If you have a cat in your life and let them outdoors, they are most likely hunting. This leads to the death and suffering of wild animals, as well as the diminishment of species whose populations are under threat. Allowing cats outdoors also places both them and others at risk for accidents, fights, and infectious diseases. However, if you keep your cat strictly indoors, your cat's needs for a flourishing life might be impacted because cats evolved for the outdoors.

If you elect to neuter your cat to reduce the risk of fighting, roaming, and breeding, the neutered cat is impacted by experiencing pain and not being able to live out the full potential of evolution's call to reproduce. Vaccinations are also momentarily painful, and in some cases can have long-term repercussions.

Feeding your cat also causes harm. Most likely your cat eats commercial cat food that contains animal protein. A large percentage of store-bought cat food contains fish meal, which means fish suffer and die, and the oceans' populations of fish are put at risk. Other animal protein comes from industrial farms where animals, such as cows and pigs, also experience pain and suffering.

Bird Feeders and Maleficence

Even feeding wild birds using "bird food" has layers of complex consequences. The food placed in the feeders is grown, often intensively, after replacing native habitat. It typically employs the use of pesticides and herbicides. The food might also have been transported long distances, adding to climate change with the use of petroleum products. Bird feeders themselves are also often a source of infectious disease, even when cleaned thoroughly. Furthermore, predatory birds and other animals, such as cats, often visit to secure their own prey. Poor placement of bird feeders can also increase the risk of death, not only due to predation but also window strikes as birds fly to and from feeders.

Knowing how easy it is to cause harm, we strive to adopt the precautionary principle that our actions will likely cause harm. We seek to never rend a single fragile thread in the web of life unless for extreme necessity. We look not to harm, but to maximize the good that our one single action can produce. To do this, we become detectives who discover how we are connected to beneficence and maleficence by knowing our ecology and being prepared to accept the reality of our interactions.

In a sense, we put on our scientist hats and our impartial observer robes as we minimize preconceived notions of "wrongdoing" and "rightdoing." The goal is not to look for blame, but to see how interrelated we are to the world with each breath, thought, and action. By looking for relationships, we enforce the reality of how we belong on this planet, for better or worse. In the long run, holding this awareness will not only benefit others but also ourselves, for we are all interconnected.

EcI Is Awareness of Interconnecting Benefit

When one individual or species is nurtured, these actions positively impact a plethora of species and ecological niches. This is known as interdependent beneficence. One example is top carnivores involved in trophic cascades. Trophic cascades are the changes made to an ecosystem by adding, removing, or changing the behavior of top predators in a food web, which then impacts other predators, herbivores, and plants.

For instance, as mentioned earlier, when sea otters hunt sea urchins, this helps keep kelp forests healthy because sea urchins graze on kelp. If sea otters were to disappear, sea urchins would overgraze and the ecosystem would crash. This trophic cascade impacts a wide variety of species, including humans, as kelp forests help buffer the impact of waves and currents in coastal areas.

Humans, too, can offer benefits to many other species in one fell swoop. For example, humans may have hunted with early wolves, who in turn benefited and then contributed to ecosystems through their impact on prey species, who further impacted plant systems.

Awareness of Benefit and Harm Helps Us Embrace Reality

Birding helps us embrace reality, not just of the world of birds but of all existence. In the movie *The Thin Red Line*, a World War II soldier in the South Pacific discovers a dying parrot chick blown from her nest by bombs that destroy plant and animal life. He muses, "One man looks at a dying bird and thinks there's nothing but answerable pain. ... Another man sees that same bird and feels the glory, feels something smiling through it."[2]

We embrace reality not to torture ourselves but to nurture ourselves and others. Meredith Garmon explains such nurturing this way: "Reality is never depressing. Being in denial, being out of touch with reality, pushing it out of consciousness so that it has to sneak around, come at you from behind and crawl up your back — for reality eventually finds a way to get through to us — that's the source of depression. Struggling to resist irresistible reality is what triggers depression and stress. Reality is never depressing."[3]

It is challenging for humans in industrialized regions to adopt an ecospiritual imperative to connect spiritually to nature in a way that would empower us to preserve Earth. As a result, we face the ecospiritual challenge to fashion what life we can on this changing Earth. The ecospiritual challenge is to walk a third way: not denying the reality we face and not retreating into everyone-for-themselves survivalism. It is the path of open-eyed and open-eared awareness, the path of connection to both nature and neighbor, unafraid to face reality and not avoiding knowledge because it's depressing and we'd rather not think about it. Garmon explains, "The ecospiritual challenge is to choose neither despair nor defense but a new sense of community."[3]

This "new community" is one in which all belong and are connected and interdependent on each other, and on the entire web of life. Birding brings us into a community and welcomes us to the family of life, which is a source of infinite wonder. Wonder is one way that enables us to face the harshness of this life, and it is a gift from the whole of Earth that transcends our consciousness.

A World of Wonder

By being honest with ourselves and learning about others, we live authentically and flow with the reality of the world instead of being imprisoned by a culture's concept of other species. We learn about our connections to others through our common roots of stardust, DNA, and shared needs. We all want to live and seek life fully so we can experience profound belonging and awe. We are invited into a living world where wonder and life-affirming relationships are possible at every moment.

When we watch birds, we nurture ourselves and grow our capacity to nurture others. Even as we walk through an urban setting, we can observe the throngs of other beings and contemplate that life is more than a superficial glance that writes off others as being a drab species in a desert of biodiversity. Mary Oliver exemplifies this in an excerpt from her poem "Starlings in Winter."

> [T]hey are acrobats
> in the freezing wind...
> and you watch
> and you try
> but you simply can't imagine
> how they do it..
> this wheel of many parts, that can rise and spin
> over and over again,
> full of gorgeous life.

Working for Wonder

Wonders happen all around us. Hundreds of wonder-producing events are available to us in a single week, and people report having an average of three awe-inspiring experiences a week.[5] We can cultivate more experiences of wonder, the basic template for developing wonder is hardwired into us. Jane Goodall was observing chimpanzees in Gombe when she noticed a male chimp gesturing excitedly at a beautiful waterfall. He perched on a rock and gaped at the flowing torrents of water for a good ten minutes. Goodall and her team saw such responses on several occasions. She concluded that chimps have a sense of wonder and speculated about a nascent form of spirituality in our simian cousins.[6]

We evolved for wonder because it helps us connect to that which is good. Wonder, like other emotions, evolved as a motivator to help us move towards satisfaction and benefit, and away from discomfort and harm. It helps us regulate all our emotions.[7] The classic example is of a bear — at least, classic to those of us who have lived in Alaska, where all life can be distilled to bear stories or bear metaphors. Wonder draws us to the woods in hopes of seeing a bear, while fear keeps us distant. Too much fear and we never go out; too much wonder and we are lunch. Wonder, when tempered with all our other emotional tools, asks us to take a middle way — to get out and take some risks, but not too many.

With wonder we connect, and life's possibilities open up before us. Wonder helps us engage with the world in ways that confirm the reality that beauty is ever present. It also helps us face the harsher realities of harm, illness, death, disappointment, and massive suffering. Without wonder, we risk ourselves to life, living shallow lives with less intimacy and vibrancy.

One study showed how wonder opens us up. Researchers took youth and veterans rafting.[8] A week later, the participants reported being more engaged with and curious about the world. Wonder also lifts depression. Another study demonstrated that people who experience wonder have less bodily inflammation, as measured in their saliva.[9]

Wonder also helps our prosocial behaviors — we become more empathetic, humble, and generous. When we have more empathy, others more easily resonate with us and our relationships improve. Our self-identity shifts from feeling like we are separate selves to being part of the whole, or even being the whole itself. By merely writing about awe, we become kinder and more compassionate, and this can extend to other species and the biotic community as a whole. Life in this world needs all the help we can get (and give), and two primary aspects of human nature that we can nurture in order to be able to help are wonder and its partner, empathy.

There are many ways to nurture wonder. As the Sufi poet Rumi wrote in a poem,

> *Let the beauty you love be what you do.*
> *There are hundreds of ways to kneel and kiss the ground.*[10]

Let's consider four different ways to nurture wonder that One Earth Conservation teaches in our Wild Walks with people of all ages.

Wow Experiences

One way to have a wow experience is to get out into nature, where wonder arises spontaneously and often. For example, as mentioned earlier in the book, I led a multigenerational bird tour once in New Mexico with one of our congregations. The children were hesitant and slightly disengaged, especially a boy named Kenny. During our hike, we saw a field full of snow geese that were bright white in the sun. Suddenly they all took to the air as their wings vibrated to the very depths of our bodies. The children transformed; they came alive to pure joy and connection, especially Kenny who jumped, danced, cried out, and ran to his grandparents to share the wonder. Kenny (and all of us, really) had encountered a wow experience!

Nature is full of unexpected and surprising events that we cannot foresee, and this is good for us. James Austin, a neurologist whom I have mentioned before, encourages us to have experience in nature to help integrate our neurological processing and contribute to mindfulness, attention, and gratitude. He particularly suggests looking up, and gives many examples of how this can wire us for presence.[11]

In one of his books, he included an event that happened to me years ago before I was a minister. I was studying parrot nests in Guatemala with my guide, a local Guatemalan. We weren't seeing many birds, so we talked instead. He wanted to tell me of his love for Jesus and Mary, and I put up my guard a little bit, unsure if he was proselytizing and expecting something from me that I could not give. I was disconnecting and distancing myself from him mentally when we reached the forest's edge, where the sun was just rising over the treetops in a shroud of misty fog.

Suddenly, a loud flock of parrots burst from the tree canopy. Because I was so startled, and before I knew what happened, I was on my knees in the grass weeping. Afterwards, I was a little embarrassed, but more than that I had a sudden clarity and connection to humanity and the world. I knew that when people said words like Mary and Jesus, it was like when I said birds and trees. That experience was part of my moving toward the spiritual, toward beauty, toward service, and toward an ease with religious differences as I saw the wonder moving through it all.

Dr. Austin says my experiences were not unusual.[11] Indeed, in another study, the researchers asked half their students to gaze up at trees, an activity known to evoke awe.[12] The other half turned their backs to the trees. Afterwards, researchers approached each group with questionnaires. Along the way, they pretended to trip and drop pens on the ground. The awe group picked up 10% more pens and felt less entitled to payment for their participation in the study.

Looking up is good for us, whether it is at trees, birds, or planets. Wherever you are, you can open yourself to wonder by leading with your body. Make a facial expression of awe, which is often eyes wide open, mouth agape, and eyebrows raised. Then say, "Wow!" like you mean it. If you are with others, point at something and invite others to see what you see, and together say, "Wow!" In fact, reader, look out your window now or at some living being near you, and exclaim, "WOW!"

Really? vs. Really!

Nature isn't just out there. It's everywhere, and it's in us. How do we find wonder in the ordinary, banal, and boring? In the uncomfortable, even? It's one thing to wonder at the rainbow of colors in our trees, but where is our awe when the leaves are brown and falling? Where is the wonder on the train ride into the city or in the subway while reading headlines of disaster and death? Can't there be something more to wonder at than the last audacious thing a crazy politician said? You can perhaps envision someone talking about a perceived absurd or frustrating event, rolling their eyes, and saying, "Really?" It takes practice to cultivate wonder in daily things, so our wonder isn't an overwhelmed or doubtful question, but a gentler exclamation of recognition or astonishment. So instead of a cynically uttered "really" we instead gush with a "Really!" Say it with me, "REALLY!"

To grow wonder, slow down and ask this of ordinary or routine objects in your day. How did that get here? Why is it here? If you are focusing on living beings, what are they doing and thinking? How are they connected to me and the web of life?

For example, pick something in the room where you are that you find uninteresting. If it is this book, consider the paper upon which it is written. How did it get to be here? Woody trees first evolved in the Devonian period about 360 million years ago. The appearance of trees and forests was one of the triggers for the two major extinction events in the Devonian period, when over 50% of the world's genera went extinct. Today there are three trillion trees, 400 for every human. There are more of them than us, and yet they contributed in the past to terrible, drastic climate change and major extinction events. We're not so bad, really!

This leads us to the third way of nurturing nature, seeing wonder in our own kind.

Dude

Wonder can be found in our own human species. If we could tap into the wonder of the miracle of our own existence — not just in babies, celebrities, and geniuses — what might our lives look like? What if we were to see beauty in all the faces around us all the time? When considering other humans, we might ask the following:

- How are we here at all?
- What are we thinking and feeling?
- How can we build bridges and go into space?
- How is it that we can be kind given all the challenges of life?

From my experience as a minister and conservationist, one of the biggest spiritual challenges I see is for us to recognize wonder in our own kind. In pop culture in the United States, saying "dude" can express a negative or disappointed attitude, such as in the movie, "The Big Lebowski." We need to leave behind the sense of being bored or blaming others. Instead, we can move to a softer and more grateful expression.

Say it now if a human is near you, or pick up a book, a magazine, or your phone with humans displayed and say "DUDE!" with the energy of incredulous admiration. While you say this you can give the okay sign with your thumbs up, perhaps smiling and winking in affirmation of who they are.

I'm Good

Those around you are also you. Their wonder and beauty are yours and the whole world's. We need to own how awesome our thoughts, feelings, actions, and presence in the world are. If we do not find wonder in ourselves, we shut down the possibility of marveling and connecting with all of life. Cultivating wonder with all life helps us not only to connect and heal but to become better nurturers of other species and the planet's ecosystems.

Cultivating wonder takes practice, so let's practice now. Repeat after me, "I'm good! I'M GOOD!" It is always a good idea to lead with moving your body, so take your previous Dude thumbs-up and point your thumbs at yourself. You are more than okay, you are Good!

Putting It All Together

These phrases, hand movements, and facial expressions can remind you where to look for wonder in nature and other species, in the ordinary, in humans around you, and in yourself. Let's put them all together: "WOW! REALLY? DUDE! I'M GOOD!"

Look for Wonder and Beauty Even When the Going Gets Shitty

The heartache of conservation mixes with an awe of life. I

learned slowly over the years that there is no beauty without tragedy, and beauty never dies; it is everywhere. Knowing this is both a burden and a blessing. Our hearts are ever open to the suffering and loss of vital wondrous life around us, and yet no matter the despair of our days, beauty and joy accompany us. We strive to keep our hearts open to our pain and that of others because it compels us to do inner work. That way, we have the awareness, resilience, and power to do our outer work on behalf of all the people who are caught in an unjust societal system.

We accept the tragedy so that, paradoxically, we can change it through transformative social action of any kind. It's transformative because the outer societal transformation only comes about when accompanied by an inner transformation based on beauty, tragedy, and love. We are not talking about some minor change, but a complete revamping of how we think and live. Through work and experiential immersion in beauty and love, we come out on the other side as completely different people who have shed the stories that don't result in freedom for ourselves and others.

Bathroom Beauty

For this transformation to take place, we must work to be inspired by beauty while immersed in tragedy. We look for beauty wherever we are — for instance, in the bathroom. Did you know that the bathroom is one of the greatest places for "Aha!" moments?[13] Have you experienced coming out of the bathroom a different person, somehow lighter? It's a dangerous place, not just spiritually but physically, because the bathroom is one of the most likely places for people to suffer accidents in the home.

Now imagine that the bathroom is outdoors and perched on a hill overlooking a river that divides Guyana and Brazil. A few years ago, I was in such a place, engaged in our parrot conservation project in Guyana. I took a bathroom break while the rest of the conservationists, called Parakeet Rangers, walked down to our boat. The outhouse we used had no doors and only one rusty piece of metal shielding one side. It was open to the towering tropical mountains that were jeweled with bright-yellow sun parakeets all morning, the sparkling river, and an expansive blue-blue sky that seemed to go on forever. As I got up to leave, the rotting floorboards broke on one side, and I fell partially through. The only thing that saved me from plunging into the depths of the latrine was my right leg that fell precariously between creaking, rotten boards. I was wedged in the outhouse. But what a view!

All kinds of thoughts ran through my head: *How am I going to get out without the entire floor collapsing? Should I yell for help? I am so embarrassed. Ouch, my right knee hurts. Am I going to be too lame to work today? Will I be able to finish this trip in Guyana? Aha. What a great place to get stuck, it's so beautiful here. I am blessed to be able to do this work even if it won't last forever.*

I did get myself out, and I did finish the day working, but I spent most of the next two days confined to my hammock at our camp on the river. An unlucky accident? Sure. There are no guarantees in my work, or in any of our lives. Our very homes, kitchens, stairs, and bathrooms are out to get us! But beauty never leaves us, even when it appears to.

The Wonder of Bird Poop

While attending Vanderbilt Divinity School, I had an internship at a spiritual retreat center. I was the Creation Advocate who led bird walks on school property in urban Nashville. On one walk, we saw small mounds of pigeon droppings under the eaves of one of the old buildings. I explained that what we were seeing connected people to birds through science and spirituality. I told them the white part of the poop is called urates. Birds produce very little liquid urine, and their waste concentrates into a paste. Their bodies do this because birds need to be light and not carry around extra water. In fact, they don't have bladders. The dark part of the dropping is the end product of digestion, like our bowel movements, except that the feces and urates all come out the same place, the cloaca. Birds' compact designs allow eggs and semen to come out of the cloaca too, and that's also where semen goes in to fertilize females.

I was concerned that I had overstepped the anatomy lesson or triggered disconnection by concentrating on a pile of pigeon droppings for so long. I invited reflections, and one woman said, "When looking at bird poop, I don't know how anyone cannot believe there is a God!" I saw her eyes glisten and knew that what she said was not out of irony, but in wonder.

Beauty Until the End

In *The Road*, possibly one of the most depressing books ever written, author Cormac McCarthy writes of beauty lost in a post-apocalyptic world that is dark, destroyed, and dangerous:

> "Once there were brook trout in the streams in the mountains. You could see them standing in the amber current where the white edges of their fins wimpled softly in the flow. They smelled of moss in your hand. Polished and muscular and torsional. On their backs were vermiculate patterns that were maps of the world in its becoming. Maps and mazes. Of a thing which could not be put back. Not be made right again. In the deep glens where they lived all things were older than man and they hummed of mystery."

The fish were gone, but the origins of their lives were ever present, connected to the humans who remembered them, who would work for beauty to come again to the land. One day, humans too may be gone from Earth. But in the DNA that comes after us, and in the molecules of whatever remains on Earth or in the universe, our mark has been made. We have contributed to, or at least been part of, the web of existence forever.

Beauty Everywhere

Another way to look at the five natural intelligences is to think of being in a milieu of interconnecting beauty.

- Emotional Intelligence: Be with your beautiful self
- Social Intelligence: Be with beautiful other humans
- Multispecies Intelligence: Be with beautiful other species
- Ecological Intelligence: Be in beautiful relationships
- Spiritual Intelligence: Be one with the beautiful all

EcI is about striving to connect awareness and body intelligence to the beauty of accepting the inherent harm and tragedy in life. In this world there is no beauty without tragedy and no tragedy without beauty. Living with this reality as we gain acceptance of it increases our choices of how to react to circumstances and might increase new possibilities for more of us to live well. By considering the needs of all, we affirm that not only do the individuals within ecosystems have inherent worth and dignity, but the entire system does as well. EcI helps us not only affirm others but all of existence. And in so doing, we live deeply knowing that all belong, including ourselves.

Ecological Empathy

Ecological empathy is an embodied, subconscious knowing that we belong, matter, and are heard and seen. It is also recognizing that others belong, and in this awareness we may find ourselves dancing to the symphony of life where everything belongs and matters. We have seen that the more we live around avian diversity, the higher humans score in life satisfaction. The birds fluttering overhead, often beyond our daily conscious recognition, confirm the interconnecting beauty between us and the world as if we are held by wings.

The same phenomenon happens when we are around water.[14] People report greater positive affect and higher perceived restorativeness with either natural or built water scenes.[15] This is also true of when we are around other animals and plants. Patients in hospitals heal faster if they can see trees,[16] and experience overall improved health.[17] Studies have shown that a higher concentration of trees in an urban setting reduces stress and crime rates, promotes healing, improves cognition and attention, contributes to happiness, and improves general mood and health with better air quality.[18]

In the practice of Forest Bathing,[19] where guides take people to areas with a high density of trees, health benefits are frequently recorded. Not all the mechanisms of this effect are known, but they certainly include the beneficial inhalation of tree pheromones known as terpenes. Being in nature can also increase our body esteem. All these experiences of health benefits and connection with the broader world of species occur at a subconscious level. Walking in nature also has a plethora of specific health benefits, which can occur even if you don't feel like going for a walk.[20-22]

When my spouse and I moved to Minnesota for one year and asked how one deals with the long, dark, cold winters, the advice we received was, "You just have to get out in it." So, we did. We would bundle up in so many layers that we could barely move and head to the river in our urban neighborhood. We saw waterfowl, the frozen sheet of ice on the lake (and sometimes frozen, deceased geese), and snow falling in the dark on the trees. The harshness of life invigorated us, as did the ever-present beauty.

That advice is the same advice this book offers: just put the book down and go outside. Even if there aren't many birds, if you move among trees and look up, your body will feel belonging and connection. These benefits can in turn be offered to a bruised and aching world. This giving and receiving are augmented by conscious choices and practices, such as those suggested below.

Birding and Ecological Intelligence Practices

Practice 1: Take a Bird Bath

We have mentioned several times the benefits of birding, of intentionally looking for birds, even if the birds don't show up. Walking among trees and looking up is rewarding. There is benefit, however, in purposely going to where you know lots of birds will be. The immersion into diverse and plentiful wildlife is stimulating and invokes curiosity, awe, and engagement with multiple species. This is like the activity of Forest Bathing, but with an emphasis on seeking birds for healing and health. There are many places where we can do this:

- A bird feeder or bird bath in our or a neighbor's yard or at a park or nature center. Because of the impacts of every household having a bird feeder, we suggest sharing one with other households or the public.
- eBird hotspot. Use this app[23] to search for bird hotspots near you. You can then see what birds have been spotted there in the last couple of weeks or on the same date in previous years. You can pick a place where you know you will see a variety of birds.
- A public park or other space where flocks of waterfowl or pigeons gather.
- Migration paths where birds of many species are known to congregate, especially near bodies of water where birds gather on their way to and from their breeding grounds.

Once you are there:

1. Breathe deeply and scan the area for birds. Look far into the distance and very close, look up, and look down. Don't try to identify the species yet. Observe their behavior. You can stop here if you would like to, because the subconscious

impacts are already occurring. If you'd like to increase the impact, consider how different the birds are from one another. Are there different species present? What are the different individuals and species doing? On still waterways, a spotting telescope comes in handy for differentiating distant birds.
2. Now take in the other species besides birds, including humans. Observe their behavior.
3. For steps #1 and #2, imagine you are these others, such as we did during the various exercises in the previous chapter on MI.

You can extend this exercise into a more cognitive experience with the following practice.

Practice 2: Birds of a Feather Don't Always Get Along Together: Beneficence and Maleficence Part I

This exercise can be practiced anywhere and at any time. You can do it outdoors, or even when engaging in other media, such as videos and movie.

1. Choose a location and spend time there. Observe the many different species and their behaviors.
2. List all the different species you see or that you know may be present. You may not be able to identify them now, but you can use apps to aid in doing so, such as eBird, Merlin and iNaturalist.[23-25] You can also use books and the internet. To do this exercise in depth, do further research after you complete your field observations.
3. Next to each species, after observing their behavior, note what their feelings and needs might be. You can write your first impressions in your field journal and extend that later through a study of each species.
4. Are there any species that are interacting with each other? How are their interactions motivating their behavior or

intersecting with their feelings and needs? For instance, you could list the trees and note how they produce oxygen and terpenes that affect other species. You could also list the caterpillars that are eating the leaves. To capture this full experience, you could make a list, construct a table and fill in each element, or draw a picture with arrows indicating interactions.
5. When are species benefiting others and when are they harming others? Where are needs getting met and not getting met? Pay particular attention to interactions involving humans or human-derived disturbances in the location, such as parking lots, roads, or the birdwatchers themselves. If you experience discomfort, you can decide to discontinue this exercise at any time.
6. While still in the field, become still and breathe deeply. If you can, sit still and unfocus your eyes. Move from being a scientist to a nonjudgmental observer of the complex interplay between individuals and species (though it's possible to be both). Ponder the inherent worth, dignity, and beauty of each individual and species, no matter how they are involved in harm or benefit. Remember that you can choose to discontinue this exercise at any time if you feel discomfort. In fact, your response is part of this exercise: How are your feelings and needs intersecting with what you have observed and thought? You, too, are part of the interplay and dance of the ecological marvel that is life on Earth.
7. Consider yourself and your community. Does anything in this exercise suggest making a change to your own behavior or taking some next steps? (We'll be talking more about this in the last chapter, "Flying Free.") Think about where you can get support or further information regarding the weaving of needs in biotic communities.
8. If you are with others in the field, consider sharing what this experience has been like for you, and see if any requests for support or company emerge.

9. Once at home, look at your worksheet and see what information you need. How might a hawk hunting a rabbit be beneficial as well as harmful? First off, fear, pain, and death are harmful to individual rabbits. On the other hand, killing the rabbit keeps herbivore numbers down, which means that certain plants can grow and provide homes for insects and protect soil erosion. However, if rabbits become scarce, predators lose a food source. This is the time to put on your ecologist hat and learn all you can.
10. Reexamine your work and then journal or share with another what it means to be an individual and a species on this planet. What does it mean to all the other individuals? Listen to your body as it moves toward benefit and away from harm. Are there any further steps or commitments you and your companion(s) would like to undertake at this time?

Practice 3: Ecology of Maleficence and Beneficence Part II

1. Reexamine your work in the previous practice, perhaps choosing what elicits continued engagement or curiosity. You might also wish to investigate further instances where you experienced discomfort or if you noticed any behaviors you'd like to improve. Perhaps you'd like to focus on what harm others do, such as a jackal hunting a rabbit or an oil company drilling in a new area.
2. Make a list including each species. List what benefits and harms intersect with their behaviors and ecology. List as many actors as you can who are involved in an undesirable situation, and list what you believe their needs are, both met and unmet.
3. Research the situation and continue to add new actors and new needs.
4. Consider sharing your work with others. Ask them what they think it means to be one individual on this planet. What does it mean to all the other individuals? Listen to your body

as it moves toward benefit and away from harm. Are there any further steps or commitments you and your companion(s) would like to undertake at this time?

Practice 4: Feeling Ungrateful and Down? Give Yourself Presence (Presents and Senses) on a Walk

1. Pick a time to take a walk when you feel low spirited and perhaps are experiencing uncomfortable feelings regarding the status of your life or Earth. Remember, even though you may not want to go for a walk, your body still benefits.
2. Before beginning, do a few stretches to open your body to the possibility of connection.
3. Choose a route where, if possible, there are flora and fauna — not just humans and domesticated plants, although they can suffice. Also, pick a route where it is safe to look up as much as possible, avoiding hilly or uneven ground, or security risks.
4. If you are feeling reluctant, promise yourself that you will walk for only one minute. And if after one minute you'd like to continue, invite yourself for another minute. Continue for as long as feels appropriate. If you experience any "should language" in which you feel pressured to continue or to feel a certain way, go to step #5.
5. Every 30 seconds or so, pause and look up and all around. Breathe deeply. Invite yourself to continue or turn around.
6. If you think you have reached the halfway point, pause again. Invite yourself to engage your senses. Look up and around. Breathe deeply. Take one breath to listen. What or who do you hear? Take one breath to smell. What or who do you smell? Take one breath and reach out and touch something – the ground, yourself, or a plant. If there is a tree, invite yourself to touch it. Put your ear against the tree. Can you hear the sap rising or falling? Can you hear your own heartbeat? Invite yourself to hug the tree. Imagine

the tree hugs you back. If you feel comfortable and have knowledge of the plants around you, invite yourself to taste the flowers, fruits, or leaves.
7. When you have finished your walk, bow as low as you can to the life around you and in you. Is there a particular tree, bird, or other animal you wish to honor?
8. You may also end the walk with some words of thanks. Find something for which you are grateful, even in the midst of any pain and loss you might be experiencing. You may whisper, speak, shout, or sing your thanks with your arms wide open, and bow again.

Practice 5: Go for a Beauty Walk

In beauty I walk
With beauty before me I walk
With beauty behind me I walk
With beauty above me I walk
With beauty around me I walk
It has become beauty again

1. Before going for a walk, read "Walking in Beauty," a Closing Prayer from the Navajo Way Blessing Ceremony that has been abbreviated above.[26]
2. Walk silently along a path. If you do not want to walk, sit in comfort.
3. Just be, be yourself, be yourself in beauty.
4. Watch your thoughts and breathe.
5. If your thoughts stray to other matters, watch them and let them go.
6. Return to the present moment. Watch yourself moving through a world of beauty, inner and outer.
7. When you reach the midpoint of your walk, pause and look up. Look all around. Stretch out your arms. Twirl around.

Touch the ground. Sit on the ground. Roll on the ground if you can. Smile. Laugh.
8. Now turn around and walk silently back.
9. Imagine yourself to be another being you find beautiful.
10. What are they thinking, feeling, and doing?
11. What are they moving toward or away from so that they can live well? What are their needs? If your thoughts stray, watch them, and let them go.
12. After you finish walking or sitting, read the rest of the Navajo Beauty Blessing that ends this way in some versions:

With beauty before me may I walk.
With beauty behind me may I walk.
With beauty below me may I walk.
With beauty above me may I walk.
With beauty all around me may I walk.
In old age wandering on a trail of beauty, lively, may I walk.
In old age wandering on a trail of beauty, living again, may I walk.
In beauty, it is finished.

Notes

1. McCallum I. *Ecological Intelligence: Rediscovering Ourselves in Nature*. Fulcrum Publishing: Wheat Ridge, CO. 2008.
2. Geisler RM et al. The Thin Red Line. Fox Productions: Century City, CA. 1998.
3. Garmon M. Reality Is Never Depressing. The Liberal Pulpit. Last modified January 30, 2014. https://www.liberalpulpit.org/2014/01/reality-is-never-depressing.html
4. Oliver M. Starlings in Winter. *Owls and Other Fantasies: Poems and Essays*. Beacon Press: Boston, MA. 2006.
5. Stellar JE et al. Self-transcendent emotions and their social functions: compassion, gratitude, and awe bind us to others through prosociality. *Emotion Review*, 9(3). https://doi.org/10.1177/1754073916684557
6. Goodall J. Waterfall Displays. Dr. Jane Goodall and Goodall Institute USA. Accessed on November 19, 2024. https://www.youtube.com/watch?v=jjQCZClpaaY
7. Lopes S, et al. Nature can get it out of your mind: The rumination reducing effects of contact with nature and the mediating role of awe and mood. *Journal of Environmental Psychology* 71. 2020. https://doi.org/10.1016/j.jenvp.2020.101489
8. Anderson CL, et al. Awe in nature heals: Evidence from military veterans, at-risk youth, and college students. *Emotion*, 18(8). 2018. https://doi.org/10.1037/emo0000442
9. Jennifer E, et al. Positive Affect and Markers of Inflammation: Discrete Positive Emotions Predict Lower Levels of Inflammatory Cytokines. *Emotion* 15(2): 2015.
10. Rumi J (Muhammad bin Muhammad bin al-Husayn al-Khatibi al-Balkhi al-Bakri). In Barks C, et al (translators). *The Essential Rumi*. Harper Books: New York, NY. 2004.
11. Austin J. *Living Zen Remindfully*. MIT Press: Cambridge, MA. 2016.
12. Piff PK, et al. Awe, the small self, and prosocial behavior. *Journal of Personality and Social Psychology*, 108(6). 2015. https://doi.org/10.1037/pspi0000018
13. Ovington LA, et al. Do People Really Have Insights in the Shower? The When, Where and Who of the Aha! Moment. *J Creative Behavior* 52(1). 2018. https://doi.org/10.1002/jocb.126

14. Nichols WJ. *Blue Mind : The Surprising Science That Shows How Being Near, In, On, or Under Water Can Make You Happier, Healthier, More Connected, and Better at What You Do*. Little, Brown, and Company: New York, NY. 2014.
15. White M, et al. Blue space: The importance of water for preference, affect, and restorativeness ratings of natural and built scenes. *Journal of Environmental Psychology* 30(4). 2019. https://doi.org/10.1016/j.jenvp.2010.04.004
16. Ulrich RS. View through a window may influence recovery from surgery. *Science* 224(4647). https://pubmed.ncbi.nlm.nih.gov/6143402/
17. Ulrich RS. Health benefits of gardens in hospitals. ResearchGate. Accessed November 19, 2024. https://www.researchgate.net/publication/252307449_Health_Benefits_of_Gardens_in_Hospitals
18. Wolf KL, et al. Urban Trees and Human health: A Scoping review. *International Journal of Environmental Research and Public Health* 17(12). 2020. https://doi.org/10.3390/ijerph17124371
19. Sherwood, H. Getting back to nature: how forest bathing can make us feel better. *The Guardian*. Last modified January 8, 2018. https://www.theguardian.com/environment/2019/jun/08/forest-bathing-japanese-practice-in-west-wellbeing
20. Barton J et al. The health benefits of walking in greenspaces of high natural and heritage value. *Journal of Integrative Environmental Sciences*, 6(4). 2009. https://doi.org/10.1080/19438150903378425
21. Weir K. Nurtured by nature. *Monitor on Psychology*, 51(3). 2020. https://www.apa.org/monitor/2020/04/nurtured-nature
22. Williams F. *The Nature Fix: Why Nature Makes Us Happier, Healthier, and More Creative*. W.W. Norton and Company: New York, NY. 2017.
23. eBird. Cornell Lab of Ornithology. Accessed November 15, 2024. https://ebird.org/home
24. Merlin. Cornell Lab of Ornithology. Accessed November 19, 2024. https://merlin.allaboutbirds.org/
25. iNaturalist. Accessed November 15, 2024. https://www.inaturalist.org/
26. Brown S. How to Walk in Beauty: Navajo Teachings. Last updated May 27 2023. https://navajotraditionalteachings.com/blogs/news/how-to-walk-in-beauty-navajo-teachings

Spiritual Intelligence
Birds Beyond Words

Warning Repeated

1. *If you have bought this book, return it. If you are reading this, shut the cover and go out and be with birds. If you still persist, I warned you. The beauty is in more than words, it is in birds.*
2. *This chapter is the shortest of all the intelligences. Why? Refer to the point above.*

Spiritual Intelligence Explained in Words

> *Seeing is forgetting the name of the thing one sees.*
> *– Lawrence Weshler, Seeing is Forgetting the Fame of the Thing One Sees*

We humans give words to describe wonder and connection, including spirituality. Spirituality is a broad concept that people approach from many perspectives. It is a sense of connection to something more than the daily human ego concerns, which results in a strong sense of connection to and compassion for others and the self. Sometimes people invoke a sense of sacredness, transcendence, or even non-physicality to their spiritual experiences. Spiritual intelligence (SpI) is therefore the ability to see beyond self-experience — or even human experience, stories, and projections — that results in a greater sense of interconnection to, acceptance for, and compassion for not just life but all of existence. The previous four intelligences also result in the same, so as we come to the final intelligence, we can see how they overlap in their definitions and outcomes. Higher SpI has been positively correlated to EI. In some sense, as it produces so many benefits to self and others, it is considered the heart and center of all the four other intelligences[1] (See the Five Intelligences Chart on page 23).

From a Nonviolent Communication perspective, SpI helps us understand others at the deepest level. It also helps us orient ourselves toward accepting the true cause of behavior, without judgment so that we may serve to meet the deep and true needs of others. The ultimate goal is to serve life.

In the book *Spiritual Intelligence*, Steven Benedict outlined the concept as a perspective that is ultimately concerned with the wellbeing of the universe and all who live there. Some, such as Howard Gardner, the originator of the theory of multiple intelligences, refer to this intelligence as "existential intelligence."[2] Studies over the last fifteen years[3] point to how SpI can be measured and can predict a variety of positive outcomes.[4]

In one study of nurses, a high level of SpI helped them improve their psychological wellbeing and sense of purpose in life, suggesting that it leads to greater health for them and their patients.[5] Spirituality can also influence longevity, improve emotional states and fitness, strengthen immune systems and self-confidence, and reduce the risk of disease.

From a Buddhist perspective, especially in the tradition of global spiritual leader Thich Nhat Hanh, SpI is the ability to live out the day with an embodied sense of interbeing. Though words might help explain and guide one into this state, the goal is to get beyond words and into "being," so that a compassionate response arises more easily and quickly in the often tumultuous happenings of our days, lives, and world. The world needs us to be as present as possible to the harsh realities of beauty and tragedy, so that in full presence we act from a sense of interconnecting worth and dignity with all of life. Birds can guide us on this journey toward remembering that we are always whole and always belong, as does everybody else.

Spiritual Birding

The disciple was always complaining to his Master,
"You are hiding the final secret of Zen from me."
And he would not accept the Master's denials.
One day, they were walking in the hills when they heard a bird sing.
"Did you hear that bird sing?" said the Master.
"Yes," said the disciple.
"Well, now you know that I have hidden nothing from you."
"Yes," said the disciple.

If you really heard a bird sing, if you really saw a tree ... you would know. Beyond words and concepts.
– Anthony De Mello in *Song of the Bird*

There is a plethora of writings with birds as spiritual guides, totems, and symbols, and of religious importance. There are also many books showcasing a variety of possible spiritual practices.[6] By all means, avail yourself of these, as just about anything can be a tool for growing connection and awareness as long as one enters it with intention, focus, and, indeed, lack of focus. That's not a typo.

Jim Austin, referenced in the previous chapter, says that the act of birding offers two different pathways for developing mindfulness. Let's unpack that word first. Mindfulness can mean being a nonjudgmental observer of your own thoughts and actions, and all that is happening around you. Even if you are judging your own thoughts, be aware that this judgment is also growing your mindfulness. To be aware of one's thoughts, words, and deeds is a step towards the discipline of accepting what is going on right here and now, and hence an acceptance of reality. This acceptance can foster a deep sense of belonging and connection, as well as compassion and presence, as you become life acting on behalf of all life.[7,8]

Back to Jim. As a neurophysiologist, he says that looking at birds and hearing them cause the brain to act in specific ways. He states that one part of this comes from observing a bird with the intention to identify it or understand its ecology, biology, and behavior in a concentrative style, which is focal attention. The other part is an unfocused and broad observance that gently sees the birds or hears their sounds in an open, receptive style, which is global attention. Both styles are present in Zen Buddhism and cause the brain to minimize self-centeredness. Observing birds allows the brain to integrate established pathways, both conscious and unconscious, and weave them into new webs that connect all of life, where individuals are sacred and worthy of our compassion and commitment.

If this sense of connection merges one's being with other lives in order to be embraced by reality, is there any way that one can grow one's SpI, or is it just a fluke of genetics and lived experiences? Yes and yes. Is it nature or nurture? Yes and yes. No matter how you perceive your level of SpI or whether you SpI comes from genetics or lived experience, by engaging with intent and responding to the call of beauty, we say yes to all of life. That yes is SpI.

Spiritual Intelligence Beyond Words — Solidarity

There is no doubt that Earth's systems and beings are in crisis. Humans can respond to this by withdrawing into themselves and hunkering down to guard their resources, themselves, and those close to them. But there is another way. Solutions can come from recognizing that we are all interconnected in beauty and worth, and that it matters when another being suffers! Embracing that reality means embracing a sense of solidarity with all life on this planet.

BIRDING FOR LIFE

I wrote a novel, *Prion* so I could to share a vision of solidarity in story form and show how people might come together in times of crisis and sorrow. I even imagined that *Prion* could inspire the movement that is described in the book: Unconditional Solidarity, or Solidaridad Incondicional (US/SI). In *Prion*, people join US/SI by celebrating the beauty and worth of life and mourning what has been lost. They come together in a crucible of paradoxical love, both wanting to disengage from life and embrace it. Out of these tensions comes Unconditional Solidarity, which is a vision and a belief that all life matters. It means that we help each other maintain faith that life is woven with worth, beauty, and tragedy, and we discover over and over again how life and the power of love have no bounds. Inspired by life, people make promises to particular species, ecosystems, mountains, rivers, and each other.

Solidarity also means never having to be lonely again, for we are always in solidarity with others. Timothy Morton explains this in his book *Humankind: Solidarity with Non-Human People*. All beings live in a biosphere he calls the "symbiotic real," where entities are related with ragged, haunted, and unknowable boundaries between each entity, yet we are completely reliant on one another. We need each other because we are each other. This reliance "between discrete yet deeply interrelated beings is solidarity." We humans can tweak this unavoidable and encompassing solidarity by intentionally emphasizing thoughts and actions that manifest our understanding of life as a related whole. Living in interconnection allows ordinary people to see that they live in "unordinary" times in a spectacular reality, so that they achieve extraordinary results.

But how can we have solidarity with non-humans? Does this mean we can no longer breathe because we might harm an insect in the air, or no longer eat because resources and lives of some species were sacrificed for us? There is no way to answer this with words. Morton suggests we abandon the anthropocentric idea that thinking is the leading communication mode. "Brushing against, licking or irradiating are access modes as valid (or as invalid) as thinking," he writes. To be in solidarity with all of life is to go beyond words into embodiment – to be with life in all its anguish and wonder and to consider yourself to be on Team Bird and Team Life.

All practices up to this point, as well as those that follow, are invitations to remember who you are in the web of life.

> *It is a blessing you were born.*
> *It matters what you do.*
> *Your experience of the divine is true.*
> *You don't have to go it alone.*
> – Adapted from Laila Ibrahim's *Chalice Camp Song*

Birding and Spiritual Intelligence Practices

One time, when I was recovering from a surgery that had gone awry and left me with significant pain and lack of mobility, people kept suggesting a plethora of remedies. I began to keep a list of these, none of which particularly appealed to me or were evidenced-based. But knowing the power of placebos, I picked one of them to pursue, knowing that even a placebo can result in improved outcomes. In my case it didn't, but I became fascinated by the place of placebos in our lives — so much so that my spouse and I joked about opening a placebo clinic. People would call in and we'd say, "Placebo Wellness Clinic. Pick a number between 1 and 100 for a treatment guaranteed to fix whatever ails you."

Such is the art of spiritual practice. Just pick one with which you are familiar, whether it's known as a spiritual or mindfulness practice. Even reading junk mail, if done with your heart and mind open — perhaps also accompanied by deep breaths of gratitude — might suffice. As long as you engage with intent, a miracle could unfold.

Or it won't, at least not in ways that we can perceive. However, studies indicate that those who engage in mindfulness practices show, on average, improvement in a variety of physical and mental health outcomes.[7] Those who are committed to a practice, such as meditation, outscore many others in terms of connection and compassion. Whatever practice you choose, keep in mind that many might be oriented towards only humans, and it might take some work to expand their conception of connecting to the "all" that is more than human culture and experience.

I am conflicted by the term "spiritual practice." I have certainly undertaken several in my lifetime, some quite seriously. And from all the practices I have grown my awareness, connection, acceptance, and compassion. Or maybe that's just age at work and a lifetime of accumulated awe, wonder, and sorrow. Whatever the practice has been, none has stuck as well as simply smiling when a bird comes into my field of vision. It has been the lived experience of sharing a planet with them, as well as other species including humans, that has shaped my neural wiring to what it is today. Their constant company in dreams and waking moments has lowered my boundaries between myself and birds.

Based on my experiences, I relate below some ways of being with birds that can be used as mindfulness or spiritual practices. Perhaps they will resonate with you, and perhaps you will add your own. Birds guide us in different ways, and every encounter is a gift received and given.

Whatever practice you engage in, invite yourself to follow the advice portrayed in this quote attributed to Joseph Campbell, "Don't do anything that isn't play." May you be like a child who laughs so hard that they must lie down, marveling that their experience is too full to talk about, let alone remaining standing.

> *Out beyond ideas of wrongdoing and rightdoing,*
> *there is a field. I'll meet you there.*
> *When the soul lies down in that grass,*
> *the world is too full to talk about.*
> *Ideas, language, even the phrase "each other"*
> *doesn't make any sense.*
> – Rumi, "A Great Wagon" in *The Essential Rumi*

Practice 1: Bird's Eye View

This practice can be completed merely by imagining a bird soaring high, seeing a soaring bird in a photo or video, or seeing a spiraling vulture or hawk in the sky above you. When outdoors, if you spy a bird high in the air or, even better, a kettle of migrating hawks swirling in a tower of feathered purpose, take time to watch them. Remember from EcI that looking up is good for us. Look up for as long as you can, and if you are driving, pull over so you can safely extend your imagination into being the bird. This begins as a multispecies practice where you become the bird, imagining your body moving as they do, and sensing the world as they might.

Picture yourself looking down on the land, perhaps with keen sight, seeing plants and creatures small and large. You see all their interactions, behaviors, and evidence of their lives, such as nests, burrows, and constructed human spaces without judgment. This is how life on Earth is, and as you move over the landscapes you see both the beauty and the tragedy of it all, but without these words. You do not tell a story of what you see; what you see simply is.

You begin to fly higher and higher, taking in the expanses of life and terrain below you. At one point you become the highest-flying bird, a bar-headed goose, flying over the mountains at 21,000 feet. You would see what a human sees from a passenger plane at about two-thirds to half its highest distance from the ground. At this point you cannot see individual lives or structures with any clarity. You do see coloration shifts indicating ground, trees, agricultural plots, and elevated land such as mountains. You know that life is there and taking place without you knowing particular details. But you may recall the lakeside, swamps, and fields where you were raised and perhaps where you raised young. You remember lives hatching, birthing, growing, reproducing, suffering, enjoying, and dying. By flying above them, you may feel as if you are them: not just the ones you have known, but those from the past and in the future. You cry, overcome with sorrow as well as joy, for the expanse of lived experience opens your internal vision beyond what you previously thought possible.

BIRDING FOR LIFE

Suddenly you feel lighter, liberated from the weight of your perceptions and stories, and you begin to rise ever higher and higher. Your extended wings feel the wind move over, under, and in you. Breathing deeply, you take in the molecules and atoms that have been part of Earth and life since the beginning.

At some point you become an ethereal bird, able to reach beyond the troposphere layer of Earth's atmosphere, into the stratosphere, and then into the mesosphere. Clouds and lives swirl below you as you take in the whole of Earth that is also you. You imagine wrapping your wings around Earth, loving all that is. Tilting your head, you peer into space at the moon and stars so numerous and clear. You seem so close to all of existence, yet still so far away. You move your feathers at your wing tips as if to say hello and embrace not just Earth, but the solar system, the galaxy, and the universe. You are so high now that there is no wind. Only silence and incredible beauty. You rest in this space, breathing deeply.

When you are ready, you slowly spiral down — returning to Earth, discerning ever more clearly the individual lives below you, but still with an embodied sense that they are whole and beautiful, as are you. You have never been so in love with anyone or anything before, and as you land on Earth, your body moves with compassion and peace through your days. Even when you sense pain or despair, you know these feelings are part of a living world where beauty is ever present. You see fully, and gratitude arises that everything happens with and without you, that you and all others are simultaneously participants, witnesses, and partners. You see that you were a silly goose to have placed conditions on your solidarity with all life that grounds you. Looking down, you see the sweet grass and your fellow geese's droppings and your own. You smile for it's good to be home: welcomed, and welcoming to all others.

Practice 2: Silence in the Wings

> *And as you pray in your darkness*
> *For wings to set you free*
> *You are bound to your silent legacy*
> – Melissa Ethridge in "Silent Legacy"

Many mindfulness practices incorporate silence, though perhaps interspersed with songs, guiding words, prayers, chants, etc. In Buddhism, participants are invited to watch their thoughts as they arise, notice what they are thinking, and then calm their inner chatter. This is done not through repression, but rather a gentle invitation to not judge that you have these inner thoughts and then let them go. We can bring this same intention when we watch and listen to birds. You can also do this when watching a video, such as a live web cam, if you cannot look out a window or go outside.

There are many ways to begin. You can purposely situate yourself where you can hear birds and remain still and silent. Watch your thoughts as they arise and pay attention to your breathing and the landscapes around you. As thoughts arise, let them gently go. You can use the sound or sight of birds to remind you to release your inner chatter, take a deep breath and begin again. You can do this for one minute or for many.

You can also go about your daily routine or on a bird walk, perhaps even with others. When you hear a bird call or see one flying over, purposely take a deep breath and still your thoughts. You can do this for just a few seconds, then return to scrambling to try to identify the bird or take a picture. Invite yourself to do an entire walk or birding session in this way, leaving behind the apps, books, and technology. Instead, breathe deeply, stilling yourself so that you imagine hearing the rush of wind as the birds pass by.

BIRDING FOR LIFE

Practice 3: High Flying Blessing

Someone once told me that every time a vulture passes over you it's a blessing because they soar on the current of life and death. Ecologically speaking, we know that they forage on the dead and recycle death into life. Some people are uncomfortable with how vultures remind us of death and decay. If we can see their beauty and the important ecological services they perform, however, we might gain acceptance that we too cannot escape death or extend our future brief moments on Earth. Vultures tell us that we are forever a part of this Earth.

When you see a vulture soaring above you, or perhaps a hawk or other bird, take a moment to breathe deeply. Say to yourself: I am the beautiful whole, embraced by and embracing the beautiful whole. If you are ready, imagine yourself dead or dying and see how this too is beauty, and it is a gift to be part of life with all other beings. In your breathing, living, and dying, you share molecules with those who came before you and those who will come after you. You are the beautiful whole.

Practice 4: Bird and Bell

> *The sound of the bell. The chirp of the sparrow.*
> *It's through these that one meets the true source.*
> *Seeking it someplace else is a deluded waste of effort.*
> – Ch'an Master Fenyang Shanzhao (974-1024)

In one of our Unitarian Universalist congregations, we had a segment of the service where bird song was interspersed with the ringing of a bell. There is a video that accompanies this moment, and various birds and bells from around the world sing and ring out over the gathered. It is at once both beautiful and silly, because some of these birds are just so vociferous, and so many bells are astounding in shape and function. It is a moment of light and joy. It is also a moment when the auditory stimulus can aid us in coming into the present moment. We may even experience the mental integration that is part of mindfulness practices that also use sound. Buddhist literature describes enlightenment as occurring when not just seeing birds but hearing them, as well as hearing bells and other sounds.

To experience this, you can ring a bell when outside listening to bird song. You can also do so by playing recordings of bells and birds.[9] Or, more simply, you can also just step outside and listen. When you hear a bird, take a deep breath and still your thoughts. The bird is calling you to take in this moment. And for those who live where actual bellbirds range, you are doubly blessed, for their surrounding sound echoes so strongly that you can't help but experience the wonder of all the life around you.

Practice 5: Journaling

Journaling about various methods are used in a variety of spiritual and mental health practices. Journaling our daily gratitudes, studies have shown, leads to increased satisfaction and compassion.[10,11] Writing down intentional, positive statements or reframing our thoughts into different modes of expression can open us up to new ways of thinking. Noting our daily activities also gives us a "bird's eye view" of our own thoughts, words, and actions. This develops our ability to be nonjudgmental presences, not just in our own lives, but with of all life. Nature journaling mixed with gratitude can also lead to greater life satisfaction and connection to nature, as well as concern for and action to aid the environment.[12] The Transcendentalists in North America, such as Ralph Waldo Emerson, were famous for this practice, especially in terms of writing about the natural world. In one sense, they distanced themselves from words by moving in nature, but also shared their transcendental imagination that fused God and Nature through writing.

There are many approaches to nature journaling.[13] Bird journaling can combine all these various journaling attributes as well as benefits. Here are some ideas for your journal:

1. Every day, write down what birds you have seen and what emotions or thoughts they elicited in you. Perhaps instead of a list, you would like to write about just one encounter. In what ways do they reveal beauty, tragedy, and the interconnection of all life? How are you grateful for them? After writing for the day, breathe deeply for a minute and see what thoughts and feelings arise in you, and then let them go. Before writing the next time, reread what you wrote the day before and breathe deeply again.
2. Make your journal into a scrapbook where you write down quotes and sayings you have heard about birds. You can also draw birds that you have seen or write poems about them. Alternatively, you can include photos, cutouts, or poems of birds that you have come across. Take a moment to review your creation and breathe deeply. What thoughts and feelings arise in you?
3. Consider sharing your journal and what these experiences mean for you, for other people, and for all of life.

Practice 6: Nature, Bird Prose and Poetry

Similar to journaling is the practice of reading prose and poetry and reflecting on what they evoke in us. This practice works well in a group, where we can share reflections and discussion questions.

There are many resources for bird prose and poetry. One source in particular stands out, which is the work of Mary Oliver. I made it a practice to read one poem a day for many months until I had read all her writings. Each day I reflected on what it meant to me and posted reflection questions on my blog, "A Year's Risings with Mary Oliver." You may find these posts helpful for your poetry practice.[14]

Notes

1. Singh MP, Sinha J. Impact of spiritual intelligence on quality of life. *International Journal of Scientific and Research Publications* 3(5). 2013. Accessed November 15, 2024. https://citeseerx.ist.psu.edu/document?repid=rep1&type=pdf&doi=9bf0ff0ff6089c81be3a506d202501dc758599f2
2. Garnder H. Multiple Intelligences: New Horizons in Theory and Practice. Basic Books: New York, Y. 2006.
3. Srivastava P. Spiritual intelligence: An overview. *Inter Journal of Multidisciplinary Research and Development* 3(3). 2016.
4. King DB, Decicco TL. A Viable Model and Self-Report Measure of Spiritual Intelligence. *International Journal of Transpersonal Studies* 28(1). 2009. https://digitalcommons.ciis.edu/cgi/viewcontent.cgi?article=1166&context=ijts-transpersonalstudies
5. Sahebalzamani M, et al. The relationship between spiritual intelligence with psychological wellbeing and purpose in life of nurses. *Iranian Journal of Nursing and Midwifery Research* 18(1). 2013. https://www.ncbi.nlm.nih.gov/pmc/articles/PMC3748553/
6. Alexander S (ed). *Everyday Spiritual Practice: Simple Pathways for Enriching Your Life*. Skinner House Books: Boston, MA. 2001.
7. Schreiner I, Malcolm JP. The benefits of mindfulness meditation: Changes in emotional states of depression, anxiety, and stress. *Behaviour Change* 25(3). 2008. doi:10.1375/bech.25.3.156
8. Conversano C, et al. Mindfulness, compassion, and self-compassion among health care professionals: What's new? A systematic review. *Psychopathology* 11. 2020. https://doi.org/10.3389/fpsyg.2020.01683
9. Bell and Bird. One Earth Conservation. Accessed November 18, 2024. https://youtube.com/playlist?list=PLT3f4GhFgYKhpINioud_nbGj4Q3HGPgwz&si=CxHQBBHBw6hLGT6U
10. O'Connell BH, et al. Feeling thanks and saying thanks: A randomized controlled trial examining if and how socially oriented gratitude journals work. *Journal of Clinical Psychology*. Last modified March 6, 2017. https://doi.org/10.1002/jclp.22469
11. Davis DE, et al. Thankful for the little things: A meta-analysis of gratitude interventions. *Journal of Counseling Psychology* 63(1). 2016. https://doi.org/10.1037/cou0000107

12. Samus A, et al. How to increase nature connectedness? Effectiveness and mechanisms of a gratitude journal intervention. *People and Nature*. Last modified October 25, 2024. https://doi.org/10.1002/pan3.10735
13. Diciurcio SR. *Dwelling in Wonder: Nature Journaling as a Spiritual Practice*. DartFrog Books: Charlotte, NC. 2024.
14. Joyner L. "A Year's Rising with Mary Oliver. Last modified July 7, 2016. https://yearsrisingmaryoliver.blogspot.com/

Flying Free
Flying Lessons for Giving a Flock

Instructions for living a life:
Pay attention.
Be astonished.
Tell about it.
  - Excerpt from Mary Oliver's "Sometimes"[1]

We have arrived at the final section of the book that builds upon the five intelligences. Now comes the time to act on your gained connection, awareness, and resilience: to communicate about birds, their relationships to you, their status, and what they need through either words or actions. In the first section, I said just put this book down and go experience birds, and they will tell you what you need to know. I advise you once again to put down the book and go do it.

If you are reading this now, you still have the book in your hands. Since you are still here, and for the aim of building community and possibly inspiring your process, I offer tidbits from the lessons I have learned during my life with birds so we can move forward together.

Making a Flight Plan

Humans and birds fly a bit differently from one another, and in different directions, just as birds speak to others in their own ways. Our flight pattern also depends on with whom we fly. As in a starling murmuration, how we ride upon life's currents depends on what the ones next to us are doing. In reality, we don't make a flight plan by ourselves but with others — and, of course, with birds. The more we slow down and listen to what birds are telling us, the more clearly we know what our work to do is.

The message that birds impart to us becomes clearer and clearer (except when it doesn't). Perhaps they impart a general direction to head towards, but what we do exactly with our wings to liberate others is a creative pursuit that could change in an instant. Whatever we do, it will be like a dance in the air, like the starling flock. Though we may change directions a thousand times, we are there to keep others safe by flying until we all come home to roost.

> *Today, like every other day,*
> *we wake up empty and frightened.*
> *Don't open the door to the study and begin reading.*
> *Take down a musical instrument.*
> *Let the beauty we love be what we do.*
> *There are hundreds of ways to kneel and kiss the ground.*
>
> —Rumi[2]

There are more ways to respond to the beauty of the birds than there are species of birds (over ten thousand!). Every day, get up and ask yourself what you will do with your life for all the precious beings around you. Then, do it.

BIRDING FOR LIFE

To Save or to Savor, That Is the Question

Not every bird flies, and those that do don't always. There are times for growth, rest, incubation, social interactions, and nourishment, for there is a time and place for the tools suggested by the five intelligences we covered. There is a natural tension between inner preparation and action. Are we to spend all day "idling" in nature, becoming recluses in prayer, meditating endlessly, beating the drums, singing, or dancing ecstatically? Or should we take concrete actions to diminish suffering and enact justice in our societies? Yes, to the last choice. And to the first.

> *I arise in the morning torn between a desire to improve (or save) the world and a desire to enjoy (or savor) the world. This makes it hard to plan the day.*
> – E.B White[3]

Actually, there is no sharp break between enjoyment and action, for they form a feedback loop with each other. The more we enjoy this world, perhaps the more we can care for it. The more we care, the greater our wonder and joy my be. Action, contemplation, and the ever present need to practice coexist. At first, our practices and action might be constructed with intention and repetition, but as time passes, our compassion arises and enacts more seamlessly. We find joy and contemplation in the action and realize that our connecting practices constitute justice by making efforts on behalf of others.

Am I Lazy If I Don't Commit to Action?

The fictional story of Lazy An in a book describing a Tarot card deck captures the tension between saving and savoring.[4] Lazy An was mesmerized by birds and so still in his observation of them that they gathered around and on him. He would spend hours in the field protecting the village oxen, so he said, but in the villagers' eyes he was lazy. Yet his joy in the birds transferred to the villagers, who became more caring of one another, the birds, and other wildlife. His "laziness" and birdwatching fortified not just his own connection to life, but others' as well, resulting in more care and compassion. Soon other villages learned of this peaceful community, and they too took up watching birds for joy. The region became known for its long-standing peace and equity among its members.

Which Comes First, Reflection or Action?

Taking concrete action does not mean leaving behind the practice of connecting to birds, nor does enjoying birds limit our concrete actions in the world. Indeed, any action, especially ones done with intention and reflection, become part of our birding for life practice. Social and biotic community justice and care cannot be teased apart from our love of this life. Parker Palmer wrote, "As we act, we not only express what is in us, and help give shape to the world; we also receive what is outside us and reshape our inner lives."[5]

As we grow our love of Earth, we work harder to put our love into action, which in turn causes us to fall deeper in love. In my own life, I often reflect that I can hardly bear to carry the burden of my love for life on this planet, wanting to escape the toiling and witnessing of suffering in my avian conservation work. But then love surprises me, burning deeper into my being — in fact, seeming to erase it — as each year I become more like one more bird in the flock. I sense less isolation and loneliness. My awareness and acceptance of the web of life increases with all its beauty and tragedy.

Most of my changes came through grace, which means who I am is nothing that I have earned. At the same time, the self that I imagine I am, and who is a complex community of cells and neural-wired relationships, intentionality has slowly seeped in to make a difference over the years. The tweaking of our lives with intention is the reason for the first section of this book on natural intelligences.

The real gift, and a hugely fortuitous one, is that I have been able to enact my love in the world as minister and parrot conservationist because I was born with the genetics, cultural upbringing, education, and privilege that allowed me to take advantage of my location, and have stayed healthy long enough for Earth's investment in me to continue to grow my love and engagement. The very ability to grow and act upon a blooming love has done much to lessen my paralyzing despair, because action is a healer of such states. Others' journeys may not be like mine, but everyone, no matter where they are on the continuum of human experience, can grow, shift, and transform, each in their own way. There are hundreds of ways to fall in love, embrace Earth, and be embraced in turn.

Communities of Ideas on Saving and Savoring

This is not work we do in isolation, but in a community of practice, reflection, and action. Many different communities have formed around ideas on how to ride the waves of jubilation and despair so that we can maximize our actions in the world. I present now a few of those communities of ideas that have inspired me.

Pedagogy of the Oppressed

Learning from nature and our response to it can be understood from a pedagogical framework. Paulo Freire, in his books *Pedagogy of the Oppressed* and *Pedagogy of Freedom*, states that life experience and prior knowledge become the text upon which to develop critical understanding and curiosity. In the case of birds, our experience with those that are different from us and being in nature becomes the text. Freire said we must engage in praxis, a cycle of action and reflection, in order to gain knowledge of our social reality and the reality of our biotic communities. This is not an individual practice, but a group practice in which people act together in their environment to critically reflect on reality and transform it through an ongoing cycle of action and reflection. Only then can humans balance self-interest with cooperation, communication, and collegiality. Critical curiosity and reflection result in freeing humans from the domination-based society that extracts and consumes to the detriment of life. The more we can expose ourselves to world-view altering experiences, the more we are able to deepen our understanding and improve our responses as caregivers for Earth. On our One Earth Conservation website you can find a guide for this process of experiencing reality and reflecting, which can be adapted to almost any activity, including birding.

Religion

Religion and spirituality can also express the basics of nature as text and how this text guides our actions. Multiple examples of this can be derived from many religions. Those that I am most familiar with, which also have some of the strongest connections to nature, include Sufism, Buddhism, and Unitarian Universalism. In every religion, however, there is an argument to be made that the given religion's views are too human-centered and have been co-opted by the powerful to assert dominion over Earth's beings and systems. Thus, there is the ever-present need to return to the five intelligences and basic relationships with life around us, and to take up practices that move us beyond words to birds. Even still, there is wisdom and metaphorical depth in religions that can help us along on our journeys.

Unitarian Universalism

In 2024, Unitarian Universalists updated the denomination's principles ("Values and Covenant"), one of which is focused on Interdependence:

> We honor the interdependent web of all existence.
> With reverence for the great web of life and with humility,
> we acknowledge our place in it. We covenant to protect
> Earth and all beings from exploitation. We will create and
> nurture sustainable relationships of care and respect,
> mutuality and justice. We will work to repair harm and
> damaged relationships.[6]

Sufism

In one branch of western Sufism, the Inayati Order, the first teaching and the most important one is nature:

> There is One Holy Book, the sacred manuscript of nature,
> the only scripture which can enlighten the reader...
> To the eye of the seer every leaf of the tree is a page of the
> holy book that contains divine revelation, and he is inspired
> every moment of his life by constantly reading and
> understanding the holy script of nature.
> – Pir-o-Murshid Hazrat Inayat Khan[7]

The symbol of this order is a winged heart, suggesting that as we empty ourselves, the human and the Divine can meet. In terms of birding for life, we grow our interconnection to life knowing that there is no "I" separate from the life around us, and thus we become whole. We reflect the whole and serve the whole. In addition, Sufis hold experiencing the divine as a transformative love, which is linked to justice and offers the hope of transforming communities for the better.

Buddhism

> Because we all share this small planet Earth we have to learn to live in harmony and peace with each other and with nature. That is not a dream, but a necessity.
> - His Holiness, the XIV Dalai Lama, in his Nobel Peace Prize Lecture[8]

Buddhism intersects with birds in a number of ways, and in Zen Buddhism birds may not be used as sacred texts but as pathways for enlightenment. There are stories of pupils achieving enlightenment after hearing a bird call, such as Zen master Ikkyu Sojun after hearing a crow.[9]

Previously, I relayed the story by Anthony De Mello in *Song of the Bird* that teaches how birds are pathways to Zen. We can find everything we need in birds if we just look hard enough, or in the case of Zen, let go of any looking and just be with birds.

Zen also asks us to look unflinchingly at reality and realize that "birders and birds are not isolated, separate selves but mere parts of a larger reality."[9] Zen practices, such as meditation and koan work, are the paths to a vision of radical interconnection that teaches compassion and vows to end suffering. There are a variety of Bodhisattva vows in various Buddhist lineages that ask for followers to take a vow to reduce suffering and harm in the world. A bodhisattva is a person who is able to reach nirvana, but delays doing so out of compassion to lessen the suffering of all beings. One example of this vow is from the Great Vow Monastery's version of Shantideva's way of the Bodhisattva.[10]

> *May I support the life of boundless untold beings. Just as does the earth, enduring a space itself. May I become doctor, nurse, and medicine for sick beings in the world. May I be the nourishment they need, until everyone is healed! May I provide for the lost and destitute everything they need, through the night to guide them. Until free from pain, may I*

be life for all beings, throughout the ends of space.
Everything I've gained, I joyfully surrender. Every step I take, I'm moving with the world. For the sake of all, I do adopt the spirit of enlightenment. And will follow the way of the Bodhisattva.

Science

Accepting your kinship with all life on Earth is not only solid science, in my view, it's also a soaring spiritual experience.
— Neil DeGrasse Tyson[11]

Science, too, has a text that aids us in our reflection and action cycle. Scientific theory asks us to test what we know, and if it doesn't hold up, adapt. It can be as transformative as Freire's pedagogy, spiritual and religious interpretations, and direct experience of nature through our emotions of awe, curiosity, and wonder. In fact, all of these can inform our process of learning about life around us, while being in a state of constant humility about what we do not yet know and perhaps can never know. But every moment spent learning and critically reflecting and adapting lowers the barriers of ignorance and human hubris that cause so much harm and instead lead to a life of joy.

Merging Approaches at One Earth Conservation

In our not-for-profit organization, One Earth Conservation we draw from many different approaches to reflection and action, and have combined them in One Earth Conservation's Vision Statement:

> One Earth Conservation invites people into a vision and practice of interbeing, based on:

1. All individuals of all species have inherent worth and dignity (all bodies are beautiful, have worth, and matter).
2. All individuals of all species are connected to each other in worth, beauty, and wellbeing.
3. We are also connected in harm. There is no beauty without tragedy. What is done to another is done to all of us.
4. Embracing this reality, humans grow in belonging to this wondrous planet and the life upon it and so embraced and nurtured we can nurture in return.
5. This reality of interbeing makes us both powerful and vulnerable. Therefore, we need each other to grow and heal as much as possible.
6. Humans are adaptable and can change, both individually and as families, organizations, communities, and societies. We can become more effective and joyful nurturers (one who nurtures any aspect of the biotic community is nurturing oneself as well as one's neighbors) and naturers (one who cherishes nature and seeks opportunities to understand, experience, and be nourished by nature). This is hard, deep, intentional, and a lifetime's work.

Whether we approach the revelatory aspects of nature as teachers through either a pedagogical, scientific, or religious or spiritual experience, we return again and again to an embodied understanding — both conscious and subconscious — to inform not just our individual but our collective actions. Harm in this world comes through the pervasiveness of dominant-based extractive, consumerist, and power-hungry practices in our social institutions of every kind. If we are to lessen harm in this world, we must work together to reframe and rebuild the very framework of our lives that grants permission to that which divides, disconnects, and harms. One person recycling cannot stop corporations from ravaging the Amazon basin and its native people and wildlife. It is not that individual actions are not part of our birding for life practice, they are, but there is so much more we can and must do.

How Can I Help Others Fly If My Wings Are Clipped?

Perhaps the mandate of "must do" may seem to belittle the very real experience of the many who are struggling with complex physical and soul-depleting situations. Even for those having a good year, or even a good day, the casual slogan of "just do it" does not ring true, for we know hard times will come again. Yet I see those who are compromised by overwhelming situations find a way to love and care for themselves and others. There is surprising strength in the depths of life expressed in individuals.

Moses and the Promised Land

For me, important teachers of the presence of strength even under debilitating circumstances have been two parrots, Moses and Rosa. I first met Moses when he was still in an egg. His parents had claimed a conacaste tree in Guatemala to lay their eggs and raise their yellow-naped Amazon chicks. Poaching in the 1990s approached 100% of this species. It remains frequent in Guatemala and throughout the now critically endangered specie's range.

It was my turn to watch the nest one evening, and the female parrot was nowhere to be seen. When there are eggs to incubate, normally the female leaves the nest cavity for only a few minutes at a time. I repeated the watch the next night, and the next, and there were no parents. The eggs' abandonment was confirmed when we climbed the tree the next day and found two eggs partially buried in the nest litter. At the base of the tree, I studied the eggs with a bright light and could see no movement inside the egg. This came as no surprise, as I thought no eggs could survive three days without incubation. We packed the eggs in a thermal bag to autopsy much later, as we still had other nest trees to climb.

The thermal bag was left in an all-black car, with windows up in sweltering heat and humidity, until we returned from other climbs. At lunch time, I sped along an uneven dirt road to return to our home base, and halfway there I asked another climber to move the thermal bag from the Jeep's floorboards to their laps where they could be cradled without too much jostling. I needed intact eggs to see why the eggs had been abandoned and imagined that some disease could have caused their failure to hatch and subsequent abandonment. The parents may have also left because of the repeated tree climbing by poachers waiting for the eggs to hatch, since young chicks are slightly less likely to die than eggs.

In the lab at our home base, I used a bright light to illuminate the interior of the eggs. There, in my hand, a shadow of a beak moved in one egg. In the other, I could see a developing chick. The embryos were alive, though I didn't know how anything could survive abandonment, a dark, hot car, and a jarring ride home.

One of the chicks died before hatching, and I worried about the second one. But after a few more days of anxious waiting and some intricate intervention on our part, a weak chick hatched chirping!

The first week of life was tough for the young chick, but he soon grew strong and into adulthood. The project participants named him Moises (Moses) for his survival that led us into a vision of the promised land. In those dark days of prevalent violence in war-torn Guatemala, where his species was disappearing, his miraculous presence in our lives meant that perhaps his species, and ours, could survive. He showed us strength and perseverance even when there seemed to be no hope. His was the first lesson I learned on how to go on without hope because amazing things can happen if we are open to what might come. This sentiment is also expressed by the character Barbara Wilberforce in the film *Amazing Grace*, who says, "After night comes day." The film tells how the song "Amazing Grace" came to be written and how difficult the work of social justice is. It can take years to win a slow success. Many work to do so despite many challenges, such as illness and the solitude of fighting for justice, equality, and the wellbeing of life on Earth.

BIRDING FOR LIFE

Rosa Perseveres Despite Her Injuries

Rosa was a scarlet macaw who came into this world weighing maybe 20 grams, all pink with unruly yellowish down. One day, poachers broke into her home nest and pulled her screaming from the warm comfort of the place where she was safe and loved. Her parents would never see her again. Men bound her in a burlap sack so that she could be easily transported from the fields to a nearby town. No attention was given to her brokenness — which included two broken legs, a broken wing, and one dislocated wing — even though she cried in pain as she was moved clandestinely through the forest.

Luckily, government officials discovered the poachers moving Rosa and many other young parrot chicks to a small town nearby. The young chicks were in squalor, the dried corn mush they were fed had dried and fermented on their skin. The birds were confiscated and delivered into the care of Tomás Manzanares, an Indigenous leader in La Moskitia, Honduras, who worked for the forest service. He discovered that both of Rosa's legs were swollen where her bones had broken, but there were no veterinarians to care for her. Despite this, he nursed Rosa to some semblance of health.

Tomas then delivered Rosa to Anayda and her spouse Santiago, who had rescued scarlet macaws and yellow-naped Amazon parrots for more than two years in the village of Mabita. After weaning, Rosa joined the liberated flock around Mabita, though she had to be hand-carried from branch to feeding platform to porch.

I met Rosa when she was nearly nine months old, and still very sick. I thought she would die but told Anayda, "Without you, Rosa won't live." Anayda heard that as a challenge; she did not let Rosa die. She continued the treatments I had begun and never let Rosa out of her sight. She even took Rosa on her motorcycle when she went to work in her family's planting fields.

I next saw Rosa when she was two. Still dangerously thin, she had otherwise regained her health: her feathers had grown in, shiny and shockingly red, and disease was replaced with feistiness.

Rosa engaged with the world, using her beak for balance, walking hobbling steps with her bowed legs and curled feet to find food and companionship. I also spent two months with her near her fourth birthday and found in her a fierce friend. She taught me that even those who have been hurt can shine and serve.

Then a scarlet macaw named Mocoron came to the Rescue Center. He was weak, timid, and beaten down from captivity. Anayda said, "Rosa will take care of him. That is what she does with newcomers." It took all of five minutes before Rosa zeroed in on him. Within ten minutes they were preening each other, and thereafter rarely left each other's side. Mocoron was safe now under the protection of Rosa.

One day in 2016, I got a call from Santiago. "*Doctora, algo triste. Rosa murió.*" Rosa had died. She had developed a cough and was taken into Andaya's home. There was no clinic, veterinarian, or adequate medicine, and no way to know which medicine would even be appropriate as there were no laboratories to analyze samples. She died two days later.

Our love and care weren't enough. But Rosa didn't falter. She lived in pain, and her unique and precious life gave us and the other macaws companionship. She taught us the kind of love that tasks us to bone-deep rending and mending that never ceases. I wish my love had been enough so that Rosa would have lived longer. Love may not be enough, and this is why we learn to relax our expectations of what we might accomplish. Perhaps then we can accomplish even more, if differently, than we ever imagined we could.

Since then, Anayda has become co-director of the Rescue and Liberation Center of Mabita and saves countless parrots brought to her for care. I asked her once why she dedicated her life to caring for macaws. She said, "Once I saw Rosa, I could not let it happen anymore." The story of Rosa still motivates her to help others to this day, just as Rosa herself once did.

Motivation Combats Ubiquitous Oppression

We need motivation to change the system in which we all are embedded, where no one escapes both the harm and benefit of social structures that favor the domination of one group over another. Those with more power seek to keep it, and this lets loose a storm of oppression. We all have multiple identities that intersect with benefit and harm enacted by social structures and access to privilege. Adding to the list of my identities mentioned earlier in the book, I describe my social identities as being a human, white of European descent, cisgender, straight woman raised lower-middle class in the southern United States of America, with several university degrees, and now aging with some disability.

With some of these identities I gain privilege (human, white, born in the United States, highly educated, cisgender, straight) and with others I fall into less powerful identities (older woman with physical limitations). The iconic depiction of privilege in most of the world has been seemingly straight, white men, and this is just as true in the fields of environmentalism and conservation.

No matter who we are, we each fall on the continuum of identities that intersect with harm, benefit, oppression, and privilege. Therefore, we work hard to come to terms with our unique identities, be tender with ourselves, recognize how much we have been shaped by our identities, and consider what we can do now to move forward.

Ken Wilson, noted biocultural diversity and philanthropy consultant, identifies as a white man and says that his work is to grow awareness of his privileged position. He states that, "Decolonizing needs to be at the heart of our broader environmental transition. This includes a rebalancing towards the feminine, towards more diverse ways of knowing, towards the valuing of the collective, and ultimately with an openness to the energies and yearnings of Earth itself."[12]

Instead, we manipulate our reality to escape a personal and collective reckoning. Wilson said, "Everybody and everything else are projected responsible for every problem, and we barely hear our own hearts beat." We struggle to hear the beat of others' hearts as well.

In the Multispecies section, I spoke of exercises to connect with other life, one of which is the use of a stethoscope to hear the movement of sap in a tree or the heart of a bird, which we do when we monitor the health of wild parrot nestlings. Something shifts in people when they still themselves to listen. In that spaciousness, we come into the rhythm of life. That experience of interconnection and wholeness is not a transitory gift we place in our shopping cart or check off our bucket list; instead, we gain ever more and give ever more by acting on our awareness.

Birding and Oppression

Oppressive systems favoring one demographic over another also exist in birding. This behooves us to pay attention, so that even in sharing birds with others we do not promote oppressive structures, but instead shine light on them, bring them into our awareness, and seek to change them. A famous incident highlighted this in Central Park, New York City, in 2020. A black birdwatcher asked a white woman to leash her dog, which was the park's rules. She in turn filed a police report falsely accusing the man of threatening her and her dog. A media frenzy ensued, highlighting the frequent structural and individual racism and profiling in nature-based activities in the USA. Christian Cooper, the black man, has since written a memoir *Better Living Through Birding: Notes from a Black Man in the Natural World*, and has a National Geographic show *Extraordinary Birder*.

Layers of oppression exist in other countries as well. I was traveling with two bird guides in Suriname, both of whom were of African descent and had ancestors who had been enslaved in that country. After many long days of looking for parrots, our conversations grew more familiar, and one man told me that he was afraid of white people. That was a wake-up call for me, for I had been having a wonderful time and did not realize the tensions that were always present in our societies, even if I felt safe and welcome. My response was to challenge myself to grow more aware of the experience of those descended from enslaved peoples, and to embody that awareness in my activities around birds.

I believe that as we treat human beings well, this extends to flying beings, and vice versa. Birding is an activity with which we can embody compassionate and transformative ways of living in every encounter and with every being. Martha Harbison, vice president of the Feminist Bird Club, affirms that relating to birds isn't just about taking but about giving, too.[13] Humans benefit from birds and the places where they live, so we do our part to care for those birds. We also keep other birders in mind. The host of the *Bring Birds Back* podcast, Tenijah Hamilton, discovered her love of birds during the pandemic, and now invites listeners to not just appreciate the beauty and mystery of birds, but to take action on their behalf.[14]

Interconnecting Harm and Wellbeing

If we can improve the human condition, we are helping all of Earth's beings, according to Tomás Manzanares, who was Rosa's rescuer. I met him in 2010 just after an assassination attempt on his life. Drug traffickers and corrupt government officials were all part of the chaos that allowed invaders to steal land from the Indigenous, and Tomás had had enough. He'd reported the names of the land grabbers and illegal loggers to the authorities, who did nothing. But the men he had reported did something. Four men waited for him at the river where he took his daily bath, and each one shot him. His brother, who was nearby, scared off the men and called for help. Tomás nearly died from his wounds, but after many surgeries, he survived.

Five months after he was shot, he accompanied me on my first trip to La Moskitia, Honduras, against the advice of those who wished to keep him safe. With pistols bulging from our day packs and pockets, we journeyed to the location of the incident along the Rus Rus River. I asked him to share what had happened. He took off his shirt to show me the still-pink scars where bullets had torn his flesh, and where some bullets still remained. "Tomás," I asked, "why are you willing to risk your life to save the parrots?"

He said, "Doctora, everything is at risk. I am willing to risk everything. If the parrots don't make it, neither do my people." His wisdom has stayed with me all these years. He understood the interconnection of the harm that would kill him and his people, as well as disappear his forest and parrots.

In 2010, Tomás could not be stopped, and he indeed still cannot. He is willing to take risks to save Earth, as are many others. Since then, his brother has survived an assassination attempt, and more recently so did the two Indigenous leaders of our Honduran parrot projects. They were unharmed, but our project truck was shot up. In 2021, in Guatemala, one of the members of our conservation program was killed defending a yellow-naped Amazon parrot nest from poachers. People are dying in their attempts to maintain Earth's splendor on this planet, and the risks often falls on those with less power and privilege to take the brunt of the system's oppressive harm. Birds are a gateway to understanding the interconnecting harm that devastates the biotic community. When we bird, we bird for all lives.

There is a battle to establish the worthiness of all, and an epic struggle to turn the tables on oppression. This is no easy task, but we apes are lucky to be in great company. We belong to an earthly flock with no clear dividing line between human and bird survival, and so we are never alone when working to give back to the flock.

Choosing Freedom and Liberation

Giving back to the flock requires that we choose freedom and liberation over oppression. I have worked for liberation for all beings my entire life, and it has been a hard path, but also a freeing one. In reality, I am not so sure that my conscious choices have had much to do with the journey my life has taken — though there might have been some turning points where I actually made a conscious choice to muster the courage to keep embracing the reality that all suffering, harm, beauty, and tragedy are interconnected. Mostly, reality just knocked me over and said, "Look at me." Though hard to look at, being present to life was a relief.

Why take our heads out of the sand only to take on more work, stress, guilt, or shame than we already carry? I answer this with the words of Bryan Stevenson, attorney and executive director of the Equal Justice Initiative: "I believe that on the other side of confession is liberation." So, we all share our stories of being caught in the system of domination and oppression. We will not compete about who has more worth based on our behavior, but we listen and take the hands, paws, wings, fins, and hooves of all to strengthen our multispecies communities. Stevenson said,

> *We are all broken by something. We have all hurt someone and have been hurt. We all share the condition of brokenness even if our brokenness is not equivalent. The ways in which I have been hurt – and have hurt others – are different from the ways Jimmy Dill suffered and caused suffering. But our shared brokenness connected us. But simply punishing the broken – walking away from them or hiding them from sight – only ensures that they remain broken and we do, too.*[15]

There is no wholeness outside of our connected animality. We cannot be free or free others until we talk about the brokenness that connects us, until we talk about the abuse and use of ourselves and others in our culture of domination. We must talk of how all lives, including all species, have been harmed or imprisoned by our lack of creative imagination of what freedom would look like for all beings. A life of freedom is being able to work at your own speed and choice for meeting your needs and having the resources to choose freely. So many of the animals in our lives and around us do not have these choices. How can we offer more freedom to the animals in our lives?

I know of the tightness in the belly and the mind when we speak of animal liberation and freedom for others. I have experienced the resistance of others to liberate and be liberated, as I have resisted both myself at times. I recall how author and moral philosopher Peter Singer probably caused more arguments than nearly any other book ever printed with his book *Animal Liberation*. He tied discriminatory views to actions of discrimination and revealed how this same process is at work in speciesism, which allows us to think of other species as having inferior statuses. We see them not as individuals, but as objects and the means to fulfill our desires. Who really wants the challenging task of having difficult conversations with others? Who wants to risk being shamed or forced into changing our behavior when we are unsure if anything we do will have an impact?

We go forth even if the outcome of our pursuit for mutual liberation is unknowable. We don't know what such a world will look like, but if we don't look past the false bars that cage our lives, we won't see the possibility of what else could be. "The adjacent possible," writes science author Steven Johnson in his book *Where Good Ideas Come From*, "is a kind of shadow future, hovering on the edges of the present state of things, a map of all the ways in which the present can reinvent itself." The past and present prepare us for any number of possible futures. Depending on what groundwork has been laid and what ideas are floating around, certain new thoughts become thinkable. Johnson suggests, "The strange and beautiful truth about the adjacent possible is that its boundaries grow as you explore them." We come together to explore the possible, in freedom, for freedom.

BIRDING FOR LIFE

> *The caged bird sings*
> *with fearful trill*
> *of the things unknown*
> *but longed for still*
> *and his tune is heard*
> *on the distant hill*
> *for the caged bird*
> *sings of freedom.*
>
> – Maya Angelou[16]

We sing not just for ourselves but for everyone. In our parrot conservation work, as mentioned earlier, we have a motto, "None are free until all are free." We very much mean freedom for not just the parrots but also the Indigenous people who have lost their land, the oppressed people throughout the Americas, and the more privileged white conservationists, such as myself. There is much more tragedy than what society has taught us, and life is so much more beautiful than the stories we've told ourselves. Our work is to keep our hearts open, so that we can be graced with awareness of the beauty and the tragedy on Earth.

Such awareness means that we know what freedom looks like. Such awareness means that we continue to work so that we are liberated from anything that is not love, and we continue to work for the liberation of all. Any moments of awareness that come to us when we are able to hold it all and feel connected to all are moments where gifts come to us undeserved. Some call this grace. We cannot plan for these moments, but we can lay the foundation for them.

In the song "Parrot Girl," written about me by my friend Gene Keller,[17] he sings the questions that fuel our inner work:

> *How much love do you need?*
> *How much love can you see?*
> *How much love will set you free?*
> *How much love can you be?*

Let's ask these questions with our hearts. Grace has a way of shaping what our hearts grant us.

Choose Freedom through Commitment and Action

In the early 1900s, newfound empathy for avian creatures helped wildlife observation displace dispassionate killing. [T]he number of people interested in birds has boomed, the number of birds worldwide has steadily declined, in large part due to habitat loss and overexploitation. More and more people are in search of fewer and fewer birds. [T]he Royal Society for the Protection of Birds in the United Kingdom has more members than all U.K. political parties combined.

– Tim Birkhead[18]

Imagine what we could do together! The task before us gains more power as we come together with others in community. We are stronger together, and stronger with intention and perseverance. One way One Earth Conservation promotes commitment in parrot conservation is that we gift wrist bands in local languages and colors of local parrots. The bands say, "Parrots Fly Free," and upon donning these we make a commitment with the a large group of people to each other and the parrots they care for. We have given out over 7,000 wrist bands to parrot conservationists and supporters over the last decade.

There are many kinds of promises we can make, including this one from the Outdoorist Oath group.[10] Their Commitment Two focuses on inclusion: "I acknowledge that systemic and historic oppression is real and that hatred, discrimination, and biases marginalize people. I will actively work to ally all people in the outdoor community."

Sometimes we don't even need to say or write down what our commitment is since our work is our oath that we live every day. Our showing up in honest and open relationship with others who share our space and biotic community creates a fluid oath that begins and ends with our calling to respond to the beauty and tragedy before us.

> *I hear a call*
> *Now will I answer*
> *Forsake my all*
> *To serve another ...*
> *Fill up this life*
> *That grows more hollow*
> *Make joy reside*
> *Where there lives sorrow ...*
> *I hear a call*
> *Now will I answer*
> — EmmyLou Harris, "I Hear a Call"[20]

A commitment is always strengthened to a greater likelihood of success with practice and when said within a community. A variety of Buddhist vows can be made, and one of my favorites comes from *Shantideva's the Way of Bodhisattva*, mentioned earlier in the chapter. When I go for a walk, I sing along to the version recorded by the Great Vow Monastery. Jan Chozen Bays, an abbot of this Zen Buddhist monastery and author of *The Vow-Powered Life: A Simple Method for Living with Purpose*, says that if we can develop a strong voice, "[I]t becomes a force that continues after we die, perhaps forever." A vow points our lives in directions of service and meaning. At the end of our Birding for Life walks, we reflect about what the birds have said to us, and what commitments we might make to life in return for the joy and life we have received.

This dream has not diminished for me despite the harsh realities and despair-inducing experiences in parrot conservation. To help bolster my possible languishing, I wrote the novel *Prion: A Futuristic Fable of Parrots, Pandemics, and Promise Makers* that I introduced earlier. Like many authors, I hoped that if I wrote of a world imagined and longed for, it might actually come to be. In

Prion, I wrote about a near-future movement that comes to prominence when members make promises to life on this planet. Their promise is "Unconditional Solidarity," and in Spanish, "Solidaridad Incondicional." The acronym in English is "US," for solidarity. In Spanish, it spells "SI," a yes to life. Together the promise is US-SI, to live in ways that say to all and are said by all, yes unconditionally.

In our organization, One Earth Conservation, we ask others to take this pledge and give out stickers, patches, and wristbands to encourage promise making and commitment to all life. We join with others that love life and make this promise together. Solidarity is a great vision, though how we do it is something each of us has to work out with our communities. Tim Morton suggests "Beauty is a feeling of unconditional solidarity with things, with everything, with anything… [Beauty means] being haunted by another entity, which may or may not be me, [and] this is radically undecidable."[21]

Actions To Commit To

> *If I can stop one heart from breaking,*
> *I shall not live in vain;*
> *If I can ease one life the aching,*
> *Or cool one pain,*
> *Or help one fainting robin*
> *Unto his nest again,*
> *I shall not live in vain.*
>
> — Emily Dickinson[22]

Citizen Science – Counting Birds Because They Count on Us

There are a variety of ways to take action and express your commitment to birds.[23] My way remains to be a parrot conservationist, though I started out more specifically as a wildlife veterinarian. I never went into bird conservation and justice work because I was particularly good at watching, hearing, or identifying birds. In fact, I consider myself rather bad at all of that. I mentioned this earlier in the book to indicate that you do not have to be good at something when you seek to help others.

In my case, I was born with a paralyzed eye, so my peripheral vision is not great, and by young adulthood I developed hearing loss. On top of this, I have an injured leg and poor balance, so it is difficult to turn quickly, especially if standing in boats in rivers where much parrot counting is done in South America. And aging hasn't helped any. Not too many years ago, fellow counters kept asking me, "You don't hear the parakeets?" Finally, I had my hearing checked, and found that I had significant loss in the higher pitch ranges that smaller parrots so often chitter in. Getting hearing aids was an amazing day in my life. Suddenly, the insect and bird worlds returned to me. I could hear them again! Yet I still miss so much, and if a battery goes out while I'm counting, I can't locate the birds as I then can hear out of only one ear.

A few years ago, people kept asking me if I didn't see the birds. I knew that something wasn't quite right and went to the doctor. Sure enough, I had advanced cataracts. Again, this occurred earlier than for most people, but I have light eyes and spent decades outdoors. I recently had cataract surgeries on both eyes, and the result was like my first moments with hearing aids. The eye patches came off, and I gasped at everything vibrant, colorful, and sharp.

You'd think that with bionic help I would be good at what I do when it comes to counting parrots. Not so. On a recent trip to Suriname where all counting was done in a rocking boat during frequent rainfall, the hearing aids frequently had to come out. Then, one broke. As for *seeing* birds, I did much better, but up against a light sky I found that I had floaters in my eyes that look surprisingly like parrots high in the sky. And most of the actual birds were far and high. I counted what I could and took on the role of notetaker and data reporter as better eyes and ears called out the number of birds flying past.

This is not to say that I entirely fail at bird counting. I know the methodologies, and I know which parrots should be seen where, but I will never be the birder who asks others if they hear or see a bird when most others cannot. Some think it's humbling for me to dedicate my life to parrot conservation despite not always being "the rock star" of birding due to my sensory limitations, but that's not my calling. It might not be yours either. The benefit to birds and people alike is to be committed to the pursuit. Committed birdwatchers gain greater psychological restorative benefits than those less committed, even if they have less expertise.[24] We don't have to be rock stars. Our goal is to have birds be our center of attention, at least for a while, and counting birds is one way to focus that attention.

We need to count the birds because they count on us. For this reason, no matter our natural abilities, it matters that we pay attention to birds and tell people about what we see. There are many ways to do this. We don't have to be part of a formal conservation project or scientific study to contribute, although plenty of those exist as well. We can document data through our efforts as citizen scientists just by looking out our windows from our homes. There is an ongoing register of bird sightings on eBird that easily allows us to check boxes when we see a bird.[25] It knows our locations and records the birds we report. This goes into a massive database that serves conservationists and scientists around the world. We can also contribute through iNaturalist in a similar fashion.[26] iNaturalist lists pages of specific studies with which we can engage. And we can use eBird to contribute to the Great Backyard Bird Count.[27] If we need help identifying birds, the Merlin app is wonderful for both sounds and sightings.[29]

If someone lives where parrots are found freely flying outside of their traditional, natural community habitats after being released or escaping from captivity, they can contact us at One Earth Conservation and we will help connect them to bird conservationists in their area. Many birding groups have specific species that they monitor at various times of the year, and for over a hundred years the National Audubon Society has been organizing counts each December called the Christmas Bird Count.[28] All these ways of collecting data help birds by helping us to better understand not just their numbers and location but, their behavior as well. And ours!

For instance, to do parrot counts, we need to be able to understand their behavior to determine what, when, and where to count. We also need to know whether to count a group as a family, or possible duplicate sightings from earlier in the count. For people who don't know much about birds or about the status of birds in their area, counting helps people realize the complex and beautiful behaviors and appearances of many species. This grows their appreciation of birds, their connection to them, their understanding of the threats against them, and their commitment to protecting them.

Often when in a new area for a parrot project, we start by counting them, which helps us devise conservation plans and education and awareness aspects of conservation. Counting also helps grow the number of people interested in doing something to help the species of birds found where they live.

Daily Bird-Friendly Practices

Almost anything you can do to help an ecosystem thrive or regenerate will help birds. Reforestation programs, or even planting native trees and plants in your backyard, are a great start. The use of bird feeders is controversial in part because it uses Earth's resources to grow and move bird feed around the world, and bird feeders can be a source of disease and predation. Planting native flora is a workaround to attract birds for our enjoyment and helps both them and Earth. We can build our ideas on how to do this by moving towards marking our yards as bird friendly areas or nature reserves through Audubon's Bird Friendly Communities Initiative[30] and the National Wildlife Federation's Wildlife Habitat Certification program.[31]

Other general practices include eating low on the food chain (mostly if not all plant-based food), low consumerism (reducing travel, purchases, and home size), and reusing or recycling goods. This also pertains to having animals in our homes. Animal companions, especially our carnivorous friends, require resources to feed and care for them — resources that could be used to care for Earth. For instance, the amount of money spent on pet birds, dogs, cats, etc., in the USA alone would take care of the conservation bill for the entire world and provide resources for shortfalls in housing and water for the world's lower-income families. The way around this is to not get animal companions from breeders or from the wild, but to adopt one, or spend time with a neighbor that already companions other species. You can also look for bird-friendly coffees where the beans are not just from shade grown, organic, and fair-trade coffee farms, but are also from farms that commit to taking extra steps to protect birds and promote ecosystem health.[29]

Promoting Earth-friendly practices positively impacts birds, as does being in solidarity with people who live where the species of birds we cherish and strive to protect also live. As we replace general domination-based societal practices – such as extraction economics, inequity, and the results of the various "-isms" (such as sexism, racism, ageism, heterosexism, speciesism, and ableism that all spring from the same root) – with dignity and equity, we help all beings, especially if we make connections to the core problem of domination.

For instance, where the Indigenous leader Tomás lives in Honduras, his people are threatened by powerful, dominating, special interests, such as drug traffickers, international parrot buyers, and elites of the country. They want the local people's land and to capitalize on local wildlife for their own benefit, even though their actions hurt many. Working to end corruption and unfair economic practices helps everyone involved, certainly including birds. Unfortunately, government authorities are hard pressed to improve this situation, and until they do, conservationists cannot work safely or succeed in the long term.

At One Earth Conservation, we seek to break these ties of interconnected harm. Our programs co-emphasize the wellbeing of ecosystems, forests, and parrots, not just in our conservation projects but in the way we work together. We include the presence of birds on our Board of Directors, which encourages us to ask, "What would the parrot say?" And we created a decolonization statement with associated practices that require us to ask, "What would the people say?"

Advocacy

There are many ways to advocate for birds, both individually and with existing organizations. In North America, the Sierra Club and National Audubon Society campaign for wildlife and birds. Local chapters, as well as other organizations, also take up local issues that address protecting birds and bird habitats. As long as we have the internet to search, we can find plenty of causes that engage in the political process in order to care for birds. If you cannot find a group of people already addressing a need, start one.

Conservation

A multitude of conservation projects emphasize birds, and many operate at either the local community or larger regional level to preserve ecosystems and support human communities that care for their biotic communities. We may support projects financially, or we may volunteer (even just once), such as donating or planting trees. Or we can engage long-term by donating monthly or annually, working with a specific biotic community on a project, or doing committee or hands-on work. We may combine citizen science, advocacy, and conservation by picking an area nearby and learning about the birds there, monitoring them, and understanding what they need that we can offer. This can be done in our own backyard, an urban park, a wildlife refuge, a national park, a forest, or internationally.

Volunteering outside of our own country is also a possibility, though many of these volunteer opportunities serve the participant more than the conservation project. But if we commit to a particular international project over multiple years, we make a much greater and more meaningful contribution. Ecotourism contributes financially to local communities that seek sustainable income rather than income from harmful extractive policies. We have to balance the resource use necessary to visit far-flung sites, such as fossil fuel used for transportation, with the benefit to communities far from our homes.

Education and Awareness

> *A remedy for greed. When you can't find the bird,*
> *you want to show a bird to someone else.*
> — David White[32]

Ample opportunities exist to save the world. Our contribution could be just talking to friends and colleagues about what we learned about birds and their needs, or perhaps gifting others this book to read themselves. Or, even better, telling them to put it down and just get out there and be with birds.

Earth needs to be protected by spreading a clear and brave message about interconnected harm, including how we must change the way we perceive humans as separate from the rest of nature. We must not normalize low welfare for some life or base our shared relationships on domination and lack of interconnection. Education efforts naturally complement conservation and advocacy programs but can also be standalone. We can lead bird walks with children, families, or adults. At One Earth Conservation we offer Birding for Life walks for people of a variety of ages, as well as webinars and courses that address transformative conservation based on both inner work, i.e., transforming our own perception of the world, and outer work, i.e., transforming society.

If you'd like to lead bird walks in your area, please contact us or visit our website to learn about how to do so. These bird walks practice citizen science, such as counting species of birds. They also seek to build community, challenge our inner perceptions, and make commitments to the life that isn't only around us, but is us.

A *Birding for Life* Community

When we do Birding for Life walks, some people join us again and again, and a community naturally evolves. If you wish to develop more intentionality and start a Birding for Life Community, what that would look like is up to the members. It would evolve from relationships with birds and one another to transform the world. An example would be to first start by organizing a Birding for Life walk or a virtual sharing of how each has interacted with birds. From there the group would decide what to do, such as moving on to the practices that grow the natural intelligences and commitments to serve life. Please contact us if you'd like our support in beginning such a group.

Notes

1. Oliver M." Sometimes." In *Red Bird: Poems by Mary Oliver*. Beacon Press: Boston, MA. 2009.
2. Rumi J. (Muhammad bin Muhammad bin al-Husayn al-Khatibi al-Balkhi al-Bakri). In Barks C, et al (translators). *The Essential Rumi*. Harper Books: New York, NY. 2004.
3. White EB. *Letters of E. B. White, Revised Edition*. Harper Books: New York, NY. 2006.
4. McKie J, McKie D. *The Healing Earth Tarot: A Journey in Self-Discovery, Empowerment, and Planetary Healing*. Llewellyn Publications: St. Paul, MN. 1994.
5. Palmer P. *The Active Life: Wisdom of Work, Creativity and Caring*. Harper Books: San Francisco, CA. 1991.
6. Unitarian Universalist Bylaws. Unitarian Universalist Association. Accessed on November 20, 2024. https://www.uua.org/files/2024-09/uua_bylaws_06232024.pdf
7. Khan HI. *The Sufi Message: Way of Illumination Volume 1*. Motilal Press: New Delhi, India. 2002.
8. Dalai Lama. The 14th Dalai Lama's Nobel Lecture. Accessed on November 20, 2024. https://www.dalailama.com/messages/acceptance-speeches/nobel-peace-prize/nobel-peace-prize-nobel-lecture
9. Austin JH. Avian Zen. In *Zen-Brain Horizons: Towards a Living Zen*. MIT Press: London, England. 2014.
10. Great Vow Zen Monastery Choir. Shantideva's Way of the Bodhisattva. Songs from Great Vow Zen Monastery (Volume 1). Clatskanie, OR: Great Vow Monastery. April 16, 2020. https://gvchoir.bandcamp.com/track/shantidevas-way-of-the-bodhisattva
11. Tyson NdG. Cosmos: A Spacetime Odyssey. National Geographic. 2014. Accessed November 20, 2024. https://www.youtube.com/playlist?list=PLEUbJSilJ0U24KnlCz7KGbBKg332ZNjG-
12. Butler R. Journeying in biocultural diversity and conservation philanthropy: Q&A with Ken Wilson. *Mongabay* February 8, 2022. https://news.mongabay.com/2022/02/journeying-in-biocultural-diversity-and-conservation-philanthropy-qa-with-ken-wilson

13. Being an ethical birder. Bird note. Last modified July 4, 2022. https://www.birdnote.org/podcasts/birdnote-daily/being-ethical-birder
14. Bring birds back. Bird note. Accessed November 20, 2024. https://www.birdnote.org/podcasts/bring-birds-back
15. Stevenson B. *Just Mercy: A Story of Justice and Redemption*. One World: London, UK. 2015.
16. Angelou M. *The Complete Collected Poems of Maya Angelou*. Random House: New York, NY. 1994.
17. Keller G. Parrot Girl. One Earth Conservation. Last modified December 20, 2017. https://www.youtube.com/watch?v=j0Lyhx3Gr3M
18. Birkhead T. How bird collecting evolved into bird-watching. *Smithsonian Magazine*. August 8 2022. https://www.smithsonianmag.com/history/how-bird-collecting-evolved-into-bird-watching-180980506/
19. The Outdoorist commitments. The Outdooristoath. Accessed November 20, 2024. https://www.outdooristoath.org/about
20. Harris E. I hear a call. On The Evangelist [CD]. Nonesuch Records. 2007.
21. Morton T. *Humankind: Solidarity with Non-Human People*. Verso Books: New York, NY. 2017.
22. Dickinson E. If I Can Stop One Heart from Breaking. *Further Poems of Emily Dickinson*. Little, Brown and Company: Boston, MA. 1929.
23. Gyllenhaal A, Gyllenhaal B. *A Wing and a Prayer: The Race to Save Our Vanishing Birds*. Simon and Schuster: New York, NY. 2023.
24. Randler C. Committed bird-watchers gain greater psychological restorative benefits compared to those less committed regardless of expertise. *Ecopsychology* 14(2). 2021. https://doi.org/10.1089/eco.2021.0062
25. eBird. Cornell Lab of Ornithology. Accessed November 15, 2024. https://ebird.org/home
26. iNaturalist. Accessed November 15, 2024. https://www.inaturalist.org/
27. Great backyard count. Cornell Lab of Ornithology. Accessed November 20, 2024. https://www.birdcount.org/
28. Christmas bird count. Audubon. Accessed November 20, 2024. https://www.audubon.org/community-science/christmas-bird-count

29. How to choose bird friendly coffee. Audubon. Accessed November 20, 2024. https://www.audubon.org/news/how-choose-bird-friendly-coffee
30. Bird friendly communities. Audubon. Accessed November 20, 2024. https://www.audubon.org/section/bird-friendly-communities
31. Community wildlife habitats. National Wildlife Federation. Accessed November 20, 2024. https://communitywildlifehabitat.nwf.org/
32. White DM, Guyette SM. *Zen Birding*. O-Books: Portland, OR. 2010.

In Conclusion
With Liberating Wings

Spirit of Love, come unto me.
Deep in my soul all the mystery of creation.
Teach me to care, peace let there be;
Lead me to truth, showing forth the paths of wisdom.
Roots hold me close, wings set me free,
Spirit of Love, come to me, come to me.
— Carolyn McDade[1]

Once, while in Honduras, a film crew caught on tape one of my colleague's thoughts about the indigenous Moskito people's relationship to the scarlet macaws. He said, "They have a close and strong feeling for the scarlet macaw. They feel like they belong to the macaw. If the macaws are free, they feel free too."

He captured what I believe is in many cultures and hearts around the world. One doesn't have to be a professional ethno-ornithologist to come to a similar conclusion. One look at a bird in the air, a penguin swimming in the depths of the Southern oceans, or an ostrich running across the plains of Africa, and we feel like we are flying, swimming, or running with them. Their wild freedom is both our own as well as part of the interconnected wellbeing of life on this planet.

And birds need human individuals and societies to be as informed as possible about ever-advancing natural intelligences so that birds continue to fly, swim, and run free. Again, our motto in our conservation projects is, "None are free until all are free." And we do mean all. There is no you and me, but only us, and our goal is none other than the health and security of each and every being.

This can be a difficult pursuit for omnivores who eat plants and animals, and people who build their homes and use implements derived from once-living beings or extracted with residual harm to others. Another often repeated saying in our work is, "There is no beauty without tragedy and no tragedy without beauty." Humans and other species got to where we are in our biological and cultural evolution through the loss and suffering of countless others.

We may be inclined to throw up our hands in futility and say we and other beings are who we are because we have to harm or kill others to survive. How can others be free when there are predators and extractors in the world such as us? The cheetah may feel free running across the savanna, but how does the gazelle feel about that cheetah's swift and elegant running? Where is the freedom in predator-prey relationships, the cycle of birth and death, or the process of evolution? Aren't we all trapped in the constraints of life on Earth? Must one individual give up their life for current or future lives?

These questions are ultimately political in nature and arise from humans trying to make sense of their world order and control their resources. We want to live and live well, so we categorize the mysteries of life into understandable sound bites to make hard decisions. A religion professor once said in a Nature and Religion class that I audited, "Life is just one tragic decision after another. This is why we need one another, so we can do the least possible harm."

BIRDING FOR LIFE

Acceptance of this beauty and tragedy invites us to experience the ultimate freedom to know that no matter what we do, we are not alone, and to align our behaviors accordingly. We are both cheetah and gazelle, penguin and fish. Our essence derives from the relationships that rose out of Earth's and the universe's very beginnings. To experience this freedom means that we know of the inherent worth and dignity of every being, and that their needs and wellbeing are of ultimate concern. What is theirs is ours and everyone's. We want the birds to fly free for their wellbeing and because we are flying as well. We may also be the peregrine striking down the young parrot in flight, but we must learn to take no more than we need to survive so that the parrot flock and the peregrine family can both continue as evolution guides them. Indeed, it may even be the peregrine's prowess that demanded parrots develop their uncanny ability to think, manipulate their environment, communicate, and live in complex social arrangements.

When we pay attention to a bird's life, we actualize freedom's vision of what we might all yet become together. Shall we?

> *I do know how to pay attention..*
> *how to be idle and blessed...*
>
> *Tell me, what else should I have done?*
>
> *Tell me, what is it you plan to do*
> *With your one wild and precious life?*
> - Excerpt from Mary Oliver's "The Summer Day"[2]

I invite you to tell me how birds show you how to save and savor the many wild and precious lives, including your own.

Notes

1. McDade C. Spirit of Life. *Singing the Living Tradition Hymnbook.* Unitarian Universalist Association: Boston, MA. 1994.
2. Oliver M. "The Summer Day." *New and Selected Poems.* Beacon Press: Boston, MA. Beacon Press, Boston, MA. 1992.

Appendix - Feelings and Needs List

Feelings include emotions, mood, affect, bodily sensations, body perceptions, and bodily states. Please use this list as a starting point for determining the words that best capture your experiences and culture. There are also ample lists available on the internet, such as: The Feelings Wheel (https://feelingswheel.com/), Feelings List (https://baynvc.org/list-of-feelings/), Needs List (https://joyninja.com/downloads/needs.pdf

Feelings	Needs
Mad	Sustenance
Glad	Safety
Sad	Love
Afraid	Understanding or empathy
Disgusted	Creativity
Surprised	Recreation
Anxious	Sense of belonging
Embarrassed	Autonomy
Boredom	Meaning
Envy	

Acknowledgements

This book has been through many different forms and titles, and there have been long periods of time when my life seemed too complex and lively to consider working on a manuscript. It is to Jane that I give credit for this book, for she is my dearest company in all things bibliophilic. She edits, she writes, she encourages, and she offers solidarity and loyalty for she loves this earth's beings. Your love shines through here, cover to cover.

A bow of gratitude to Gail, who also kept asking me about the progress of the book and then took it upon herself to edit. She loves birds and we have shared many walks together, and this inspired me to finish this book.

It must run in the family, for Emma, Gail's daughter, gave the final touches of editing to this book. Her careful eye and perspective helped me see the book in a different and more encompassing way.

My deepest gratitude goes to Joyce, not only for her invaluable editing and support of the book, but also for her consistent friendship and unwavering support for the past 55 years.

I do not know what this book would be without the cover created by Rebecca. Thank you for your creative vision and patience with the finalization of this book. You gave it wings.

Meredith, my spouse, did not journey with me through all the writing, but what he contributed was spectacular, as is he. His expression of wonder as we admire birds together fills my heart, which in turn I pass on to you with these words and stories.

To the thousands of people who have accompanied me on Bird Walks, Parrot Pilgrimages, and field parrot conservation activities, I give thanks for the wonder we shared that led to this book so that others could also let joy fly.

About One Earth Conservation

This book is published by One Earth Conservation to serve birds and people everywhere. You can find out more about the book, access Bird Walk Guides, purchase associated merchandise, and learn more about One Earth by visiting our website.

One Earth is a U.S.-based 501(c)(3) not-for-profit organization that seeks to heal human systems that diminish individual worth and separate humans artificially from the rest of nature in many ways. We affirm that people must be healthy and develop multiple intelligences so that all of life on Earth can flourish. One Earth promotes parrot wellbeing in the Americas by conducting transformative parrot conservation, taking action to end the wildlife trade. Part of this mission includes encouraging people to develop a strong sense of human connection to all life, which results in the wellbeing of all. We also encourage building knowledge, motivation, resilience, and capacity in people, organizations, and communities in the United States and internationally. We do this so that they can better cherish and nurture themselves, nature, and other beings. This is achieved by combining work directed outward toward other beings (our conservation work with parrots in the Americas) and nature with work directed inward toward one's own human nature (our Nurture Nature Program), as outer wellbeing and inner wellbeing are inseparable and mutually beneficial.

To join our team, you can sign up for our e-newsletter, where we report on our work with endangered parrots in the Americas and list upcoming events and activities. We also enjoy working with volunteers who seek to serve life through One Earth, such as by helping with organizational growth, social media, and conservation. You may also join our Parrot Conservation Corps, a year-long program focused on parrots, but adaptable to working with wildlife, social justice, and conservation anywhere.

For more information, visit www.oneearthconservation.org.

About the Cover
A Birding for Life Practice

After showing drafts of the book to many people, the conversations that followed have been enlightening and deepening, compelling me to use the cover as an example of a birding for life practice.

Please join me in engaging in the questions below, which outline the five intelligences and the chapters in this book. I will then share responses and a deeper explanation of the ecology as previously covered in the book's beginning, "Praise and Explanation of the Cover of *Birding for Life*."

1. Emotional Intelligence: When you first looked at the cover what emotions arose in you? Which needs are being addressed or remain unfulfilled? Are you feeling glad, wondrous, low energy, or disappointed? Are your needs for aesthetics, belonging, wonder, understanding, and curiosity being addressed?
2. Social Intelligence: Show the cover to others and inquire about their feelings and needs. Help each other uncover more feelings, values, and needs that are important to one another.
3. Multispecies Intelligence: What are the species of birds present on the cover? What are the birds doing? What do you imagine they might be feeling and needing? What subjective experiences are occurring for them? Are they afraid, happy, relaxed? Are their care, relationship, and health needs being met? Now dig deeper to research the relationships between these two species on the cover. What is their ecology and behavior? How does this change your perception of their feelings and needs?

4. Ecological Intelligence: What are all the actors involved in this scene on the cover? What species can you observe, and which ones might be there that you can't see? What is the time of day, the climate, and the characteristics of the ecosystem? How is one species helping or harming another?
5. Spiritual Intelligence: Now let go of thinking about feelings and needs and just be an impartial observer flying over the scene, even higher than the yellow-naped Amazon parrots on the back cover. Can you imagine yourself experiencing being part of the beautiful whole, with all its complexities and tragedies? Imagine that you wrap your wings around the Earth and all beings, and you in turn are embraced. There is no right doing or wrong doing, there is just this moment with the interconnected whole. When you are ready to land, ask yourself how you responded to this "bird's-eye view." What are you feeling and needing now? (return to step #1 and repeat the steps as necessary).
6. Flying Free and Giving a Flock: Having dug deeply into experiencing the world of these birds and their ecosystem, and growing your awareness of yourself and others, are there any requests you'd like to ask of yourself or others? What might you do to serve life and fly free? How was this practice for you?

Further Explanation of the Cover

The relationship between crested caracaras and black vultures is complicated, and we are still learning. Some competition and antagonistic behavior has been observed between them but also collaboration. The behavior they display is called allopreening, the mutual grooming of feathers and skin patches. This is a common social behavior in the same species but occasionally occurs between different species, a phenomenon known as interspecific allopreening.

BIRDING FOR LIFE

On the front cover, both birds perch on dead branches overlooking low mountains and hills. Many birds prefer high perches without leaves to spot predators, find food, or locate flock mates, and where they can be observed. The same dead branches are frequently used by different species throughout the day. These dead branches and trees are essential to ecosystems, offering shelter and food for insects. In turn, other species seek exposed and decaying wood to feed on the inhabitants within. Dead trees with their often-abundant cavities provide nesting opportunities for vertebrates.

I highlight scavenger birds because they are generally undervalued compared to more colorful species. Unfortunately, human biases have resulted in the widespread killing and decline of scavenger birds in many ecosystems.

On the back cover the image of parrots flying into the sunrise is a familiar scene in my work. Often parrots' bright green colors are not evident in the early morning light. Parrots frequently leave their roosts in loud and raucous groups, and this has been a source of the wonder, sudden awareness, and connection to the world described in this book. Intent on their search for nests, food, or roosts, the birds reflect their autonomy: they are not here for our gaze but to live and fly in freedom.

In this scene that spans the entire cover, the sun emerges and the hills transition from the night's darkness and don't yet exhibit their full spectrum of colors. Early morning is often a time for quieter social interactions, such as preening, and a time to leave the roost and seek food, like the parrots. Perhaps the hills look brown because of a recent wildfire or drought, common in the natural range of these birds. Following a wildfire, black vultures and crested caracaras frequently gather to consume species that have perished or sustained injuries.

I often find myself desiring abundant green foliage, which is not in this artist's rendering. The brown hills symbolize Earth's dire state and potential desolation in our future. They remind us that our work remains unfinished.

The cover encompasses much, including challenge, mystery, and beauty. Such is the practice of being with birds. We let go of the outcomes and dance along with the unknown as we experience life's art of the impossible.

About the Author

LoraKim combines her experience as a wildlife veterinarian, Unitarian Universalist minister, and Certified Trainer in Nonviolent Communication to address the importance of both human and nonhuman wellbeing. She serves as a Community Minister affiliated with the First Unitarian Church of Des Moines, Iowa, and Co-director of One Earth Conservation. She is an inspiring speaker and leads nation-wide workshops and webinars in Compassionate Communication and Nurturing Nature. With over 38 years of experience working with parrot conservation in the Americas, she currently leads projects in Guatemala, Honduras, Nicaragua, Guyana, Suriname, and Paraguay. You can read about her life and work in her memoir, *Conservation in Time of War*.

Other Books by LoraKim Joyner

Conservation in Time of War: A Transformational Journey through Beauty and Tragedy

Nurturing Discussion: Nurturing Nature, Yourself, and Your Relationships (with co-author Gail Koelln)

Prion: A Futuristic Fable of Parrots, Pandemics, and Promise-makers

Published by One Earth Conservation

www.ingramcontent.com/pod-product-compliance
Lightning Source LLC
Chambersburg PA
CBHW020456030426
42337CB00011B/130